THE
COMPLETE
JESUS

THE
COMPLETE
JESUS

RICKY ALAN MAYOTTE

STEERFORTH PRESS

SOUTH ROYALTON, VERMONT

For information about permission to reproduce
selections from this book, write to:
Steerforth Press L.C., P.O. Box 70, South Royalton, Vermont 05068.

All verses from the Gospels of Mark and John are taken from the *New Oxford Annotated Bible*, Revised Standard Version; copyright © 1971, and used by permission of Oxford University Press.

Seventy verses from the Gospel of Matthew — all of those included in chapter IX, "Apocalyptic and Revelation," and ten of those ([44–A] through [53–A]) included in chapter VIII, "Diverse Doctrine" — are taken from the *King James Version*.

The remainder of the Gospel of Matthew (534 verses) and all of the Gospel of Luke (393 verses) are taken from the *New King James Version*; copyright © 1979, 1980, 1982 and used by permission of Thomas Nelson, Inc.

All verses from the Gnostic Gospels are taken from *The Nag Hammadi Library in English, 3rd Completely Revised Ed.* by James M. Robinson, General Editor; copyright © 1988 by E. J. Brill, Leiden, The Netherlands, reprinted by permission of HarperCollins Publishers, Inc.

Excerpts from *New Testament Apocrypha* (Volume I and II), edited by Edgar Hennecke and Wilhelm Schneemelcher; copyright © 1965 by The Lutterworth Press, published in the United States by and reprinted by permission of Westminster John Knox Press.

Library of Congress Cataloging-in-Publication Data

Mayotte, Ricky Alan, 1959–
The complete Jesus / Ricky Alan Mayotte.
p. cm.
Introduction, p. vi: " . . . a compilation of sayings and teachings attributed
to Jesus from the New Testament, Christian Gnostic writings, and
New Testament Apocrypha."
Includes bibliographical references.
ISBN 1-883642-45-0 (alk. paper)
1. Jesus Christ—Words. I. Title.
BT306.M37   1997
226' .05208—dc21   CIP
Manufactured in the United States of America

SECOND PRINTING

CONTENTS

Introduction

The Complete Jesus is a compilation of sayings and teachings attributed to Jesus from the New Testament, Christian Gnostic writings, and New Testament Apocrypha. This work is, I believe, the most complete collection of sayings attributed to Jesus in a single volume. It is intended to serve as a guide to the teachings of Jesus as they were heard and recorded by a variety of early Christian writers from different sects. For this reason I have organized the sayings according to categories of belief and teaching, rather than simply listing them by source, in the hope that in this way the words of Jesus might be read without preconception.

The purpose of this book is not to establish whether the living Jesus actually uttered all or only some of the teachings collected here — a subject of immense scholarly controversy — but rather to help us approach more closely what Jesus may have actually taught. Since Jesus himself left no written statement we must rely on the accounts and traditions of those who recorded his words and actions. The traditional Bible, of course, is an excellent place to begin our search, but what of the other writings, which are just as ancient as those we commonly refer to as scripture? For this we need to turn to the noncanonical religious writings that have come to be known as "apocrypha."

Even within the early church there was some confusion on the matter of scripture. Much of what we now call apocryphal enjoyed immense popularity among the early Christians. Although some was not considered to be as reliable as other scripture, it was still thought to be significant and important.

Scholars believe that most of these stories were handed down orally for years before being committed to paper. The scribes who recorded them were free to interpret traditional stories from the perspective of their particular sect or group. The result is that the

Gospels and other documents are a subtle and sometimes confusing mix of the actual words of Jesus and his followers, along with other material that was added later. As the Christian movement grew, the differing sects fell into conflict over doctrine and belief. Some of these groups were able to reach agreement and be absorbed into the growing orthodox church, while others held a philosophy or doctrine so diverse that they remained separate, at odds with the popular orthodox movement. Naturally each sect felt that its members were the only "true" followers of Jesus' teaching and they often had, or created, their own scripture to back them up. The Gnostics were such a sect, once numerous and found in many parts of the ancient Middle East. Who were the Christian Gnostics and why, if the sect was so popular, have most modern Christians never heard of them or their teachings?

The Gnostics were an early Christian sect that seemed to combine several different beliefs and philosophies. Their unusual views and doctrines — for example, their hostility toward the Jewish God as a false and evil god — caused them to be branded as heretics by the early orthodox church. The resulting conflict led to the eventual demise of the sect altogether. As the orthodox movement grew in popularity, Gnostics were physically driven from their communities and even killed. A death knell sounded for the Gnostic movement in the year 313 when the Roman emperors Constantine and Licinius issued the Edict of Milan commanding religious toleration throughout the Roman Empire. It is ironic that an edict of tolerance marked the beginning of the end for this religious group, but as various Christian sects began to merge and conform to one another the Gnostics became obvious in their nonconformity. Repeatedly branded as heretics by the growing orthodox sect, the Gnostics were forced underground.

The sect endured for a time on the fringes of the empire or as secret societies but eventually disappeared entirely, leaving behind only the record of angry attacks in early Christian polemics and a "library" of books hidden and forgotten in the sands of Egypt. In fact, the eradication of Gnostic beliefs and literature was so successful that almost nothing concrete was known about them until 1945, when an extensive collection of Christian Gnostic texts was discovered buried in an earthenware jar near the village of Nag Hammadi in upper Egypt.

The Gnostic Gospel of Thomas is a collection of sayings that have many parallels to the New Testament Gospels and may be related to the so called "Q document," a hypothetical work, now lost, which many scholars believe was used in the composition of the synoptic Gospels of Matthew and Luke. Many of the sayings in the Gospel of Thomas closely resemble Jesus', words in the canonical Gospels, but others are previously unknown. Some of the new sayings at least sound like the traditional Jesus, but many are strange and elusive. Had the Gnostic view of Jesus become the dominant accepted doctrine of the early church, we would have a very different Christianity than we know today.

The word "apocrypha" is used to refer to an ancient religious text that is not found in the accepted canon of scripture. The books of the New Testament were recognized as canon in almost the same form we know them today by the orthodox church by the third century c.e. All other religious writings not included in the New Testament were relegated, by their omission, to the realm of inferior religious writings we now call apocryphal writings. Although widely read among the general populace in the early Christian period, the apocryphal works were held suspect by the church hierarchy and were slowly lost or forgotten. It is to these ancient scriptures, largely forgotten by all but scholars, that we will turn our attention.

Why should we look at this alternative ancient scripture that has been attributed to Jesus? In the organization of the early church and subsequent refining and polishing of doctrine over almost two thousand years much may have been lost. Our view of Jesus has been shaded by the doctrine of modern Christianity, but what of the traditions of the other early sects, which considered themselves to be no less "Christian" then we consider ourselves today? Could not these early Christians have recorded genuine words and teachings of Jesus that have been forgotten or deliberately ignored because their scribes belonged to groups later condemned by the prevailing Christian movement?

The collection of sayings, teachings, and parables presented here have all been attributed to Jesus in ancient religious literature. Some of the material will sound hauntingly familiar and some has an almost Zen-like quality. All of the material is thought-provoking and profound. Scholars differ on which, if any, of these sayings were actually uttered by Jesus. I have made no attempt to sort out these controversies here. But the reader may be confident that whatever we know of the teachings and sayings attributed to Jesus, everything he said to us that has survived and come down to us intact can be found represented in this book.

Of course, any work that covers such a wide range of material is subject to a degree of editing. For example, the "Sayings of the Lord," found at Oxyrhynchus and now known to be fragments from the "Gospel of Thomas," is not listed as a source for this book since the Nag Hammadi version represents the work in its entirety. The "Sayings of the Lord" are so fragmented as to fall into the category of "Agrapha" or isolated sayings, and it would be confusing or redundant to repeat them. Nevertheless, there is very little that did not find its way into this book, and there is no substantive teaching of Jesus that is not represented here.

The Complete Jesus is broken into nine sections, each dealing with a specific type of teaching (Commandments, Parables, etc.). These sections have been organized by theme, not source, allowing us to view all the sayings with a common form or subject in one section.

They begin with the best known Christian teachings, the commandments and the parables, and proceed toward the least known, the "apocalyptic and revelations," which sound strange to the modern ear. This progression from the most familiar to the least familiar texts has been repeated within each section; the Gospels are quoted first, the Gnostic gospels next, and on to the little-known minor works of the ancient world. By thus leading the reader from the familiar to the strange, the essential mystery — the elusiveness of Jesus' teaching — is repeatedly emphasized.

Each saying or teaching has been numbered consecutively within each chapter and is followed by a letter, which corresponds to an appendix at the end of the book. Each appendix refers to the document from which the saying was taken, and also contains a brief description and history of that particular document. Also, by matching the number of the saying under the correct heading in the appendix (Commandments, Parables, etc.), the exact chapter and verse of each saying may be found in its original source. For example, if you would like to know more about the saying numbered [76–F] from chapter 2, "Parables," you would turn to Appendix F at the back of the book and find that F refers to the Gnostic "Gospel of Thomas," and could read the history and information pertaining to it. Furthermore, by looking under the subtitle "Parables" (the section in which the saying was found) in that appendix and finding the number of the saying [76] in the list, you would discover that this is listed as saying #45 in the accepted numbering of sayings in the Gospel of Thomas. Although it sounds complicated, it is a simple system and can be mastered in a shorter time than it takes to read these instructions.

The English versions of ancient documents in this book represent the work of many different translators at different times, who in turn were translating into English the work of many individual ancient writers. Since many different hands have rendered the various works of the Gnostic Gospels and the New Testament

Apocrypha I have also drawn on different translators for the Canonical Gospels. Most of the verses from Matthew and Luke have been taken from the New King James Version, Mark and John from the Revised Standard Version, and the Book of Revelation from the King James Version.

It should be noted that I have simplified the reference system and that some of my reference numbers will read differently from the system used by translators and scholars. For instance, a scholar's conventional reference to "The Nag Hammadi Library," VII 2:58, 23, would denote the seventh codex (VII), the second tractate (2), the page of the codex (58), and the line (23). I have used the more familiar formula of book, chapter, and verse in this manner. Instead of using the codex and tractate numbers (VII 2), I have used the title of the tractate (The Second Treatise of the Great Seth) as book, the page number (58) as chapter, and the line number (23) as verse. In this system VII 2:58,23 converts into "The Second Treatise of the Great Seth 58:23." I believe this system will be less confusing to the nonspecialist since most are already familiar with biblical referencing. This system has been used throughout and should be easily understood by all.

All of the sayings, teachings, and parables listed here have been attributed to Jesus in the document from which they were taken. Dialogue spoken by people other than Jesus has been retained in a few instances when necessary to provide a context for his words.

Chapter 7 in this book is titled "Jesus Laughing." Nowhere in the New Testament is there a report of Jesus laughing or even cracking a smile. This has been the start of many a heated debate between biblical scholars, past and present. It is only in the Gnostic scripture that we find the Savior smiling or laughing aloud. It is my own opinion that since we know "Jesus wept" (Jn 11:35), he must have also been capable of the opposite emotion. He was, after all, human. Fundamentalist friends of mine, who adhere to the non-laughing Jesus, point out that Jesus was uniformly serious due to his divine nature. This theory does not hold water with me, since I would expect one of divine nature to be a happy, joyful person. The message of Jesus was, indeed, very serious, but the picture of a savior who never laughed or smiled, to my mind, seems inhuman and un-Godlike. "Jesus Laughing" is the only chapter in this work where a direct quote attributed to Jesus is not necessary to ensure its inclusion. The report of a smile is enough.

In our quest to find the historical Jesus, the origins of doctrine, or a focal point for our own religious views, we must look at all the pieces. Although the puzzle may never be complete, each new piece brings us one step closer to understanding the whole. I believe that the portrait of Jesus that emerges in this book, unmediated by scholars or church fathers, is a commanding figure, at once familiar and strange. What he wanted to tell us can be found here.

I

Commandments

[1-A]   It is written again, 'You shall not tempt the Lord your God.'

[2-A]   'You shall worship the Lord your God, and him only you shall serve.'

[3-A]   'Repent, for the kingdom of heaven is at hand.'

[4-A]   Again you have heard that it was said to those of old, 'You shall not swear falsely, but shall perform your oaths to the Lord.' But I say to you, do not swear at all: neither by heaven, for it is God's throne; nor by the earth, for it is His footstool; nor by Jerusalem, for it is the city of the great King. Nor shall you swear by your head, because you cannot make one hair white or black. But let your 'Yes' be 'Yes,' and your 'No,' 'No.' For whatever is more than these is from the evil one.

[5–A]   You have heard that it was said, 'An eye for an eye and a tooth for a tooth.' But I tell you not to resist an evil person. But whoever slaps you on your right cheek, turn the other to him also. If anyone wants to sue you and take away your tunic, let him have your cloak also. And whoever compels you to go one mile, go with him two. Give to him who asks you, and from him who wants to borrow from you do not turn away. You have heard that it was said, 'You shall love your neighbor and hate your enemy.' But I say to you, love your enemies, bless those who curse you, do good to those who hate you, and pray for those who spitefully use you and persecute you, that you may be sons of your Father in heaven; for He makes His sun rise on the evil and on the good, and sends rain on the just and on the unjust.

[6–A]   Take heed that you do not do your charitable deeds before men, to be seen by them. Otherwise you have no reward from your Father in heaven. Therefore, when you do a charitable deed, do not sound a trumpet before you as the hypocrites do in the synagogues and in the streets, that they may have glory from men. Assuredly, I say to you, they have their reward. But when you do a charitable deed, do not let your left hand know what your right hand is doing, that your charitable deed may be in secret; and your Father who sees in secret will Himself reward you openly.

[7–A]   Judge not, that you be not judged. For with what judgment you judge, you will be judged; and with the measure you use, it will be measured back to you.

[8–A]   Do not give what is holy to the dogs; nor cast your pearls before swine, lest they trample them under their feet, and turn and tear you in pieces.

[9–A]   Do not go into the way of the Gentiles, and do not enter a city of the Samaritans. But go rather to the lost sheep of the house of Israel. And as you go, preach, saying, 'The kingdom of heaven is at hand.'

[10–A]   Whatever I tell you in the dark, speak in the light; and what you hear in the ear, preach on the housetops.

[11–A]   Take My yoke upon you and learn from Me, for I am gentle and lowly in heart, and you will find rest for your souls. For My yoke is easy and My burden is light.

[12–A]   Get behind me, Satan! You are an offense to Me, for you are not mindful of the things of God, but the things of men. *Then Jesus said to his disciples*, If anyone desires to come after Me, let him deny himself, and take up his cross, and follow Me.

[13–A]   Moreover if your brother sins against you, go and tell him his fault between you and him alone. If he hears you, you have gained your brother. But if he will not hear, take with you one or two more, that 'by the mouth of two or three witnesses every word may be established.' And if he refuses to hear them, tell it to the church. But if he refuses even to hear the church, let him be to you like a heathen and a tax collector.

[14–A]   *Jesus said*, 'You shall not murder,' 'You shall not commit adultery,' 'You shall not steal,' 'You shall not bear false witness,' 'Honor your father and your mother,' and, 'You shall love your neighbor as yourself.'
   The young man said to Him, 'All these things I have kept from my youth. What do I still lack?'
   Jesus said to him, If you want to be perfect, go, sell what you have

and give to the poor, and you will have treasure in heaven; and come, follow Me.

[15–A]   'You shall love the Lord your God with all your heart, with all your soul, and with all your mind.' This is the first and great commandment. And the second is like it: 'You shall love your neighbor as yourself.' On these two commandments hang all the Law and the Prophets.

[16–A]   But you, do not be called 'Rabbi'; for One is your Teacher, the Christ, and you are all brethren. Do not call anyone on earth your father; for One is your Father, He who is in heaven. And do not be called teachers; for One is your Teacher, the Christ. But he who is greatest among you shall be your servant.

[17–A]   Go therefore and make disciples of all the nations, baptizing them in the name of the Father and of the Son and of the Holy Spirit, teaching them to observe all things that I have commanded you; and lo, I am with you always, even to the end of the age.

[18–B]   Where you enter a house, stay there until you leave the place. And if any place will not receive you and they refuse to hear you, when you leave, shake off the dust that is on your feet for a testimony against them.

[19–B]   Let the children come to me, do not hinder them; for to such belongs the kingdom of God. Truly, I say to you, whoever does not receive the kingdom of God like a child shall not enter it.

[20–B]   You know the commandments: 'Do not kill, Do not commit adultery, Do not steal, Do not bear false witness, Do not defraud, Honor your father and mother.'

[2 I–B]   *And Jesus looking upon him loved him, and said to him,* You lack one thing; go, sell what you have, and give to the poor, and you will have treasure in heaven; and come, follow me.

[2 2–B]   *Jesus answered,* The first is, 'Hear, O Israel: The lord our God, the Lord is one; and you shall love the Lord your God with all your heart, and with all your soul, and with all your mind, and with all your strength.' The second is this, 'You shall love your neighbor as yourself.' There is no other commandment greater than these.

[2 3–B]   Go into all the world and preach the gospel to the whole creation.

[2 4–C]   *And Jesus answered and said to him,* Get behind Me, Satan! For it is written, 'You shall worship the Lord your God, and Him only you shall serve.'

[2 5–C]   But I say to you who hear: Love your enemies, do good to those who hate you, bless those who curse you, and pray for those who spitefully use you. To him who strikes you on the one cheek, offer the other also. And from him who takes away your cloak, do not withold your tunic either. Give to everyone who asks of you. And from him who takes away your goods do not ask them back. And just as you want men to do to you, you also do to them likewise. But if you love those who love you, what credit is that to you? For even sinners love those who love them. And if you do good to those who do good to you, what credit is that to you? For even sinners do the same. And if you lend to those from whom you hope to recieve back, what credit is that to you? For even sinners lend to sinners to receive as much back.

[26-C]   But love your enemies, do good, and lend, hoping for nothing in return; and your reward will be great, and you will be sons of the Most High. For He is kind to the unthankful and evil. Therefore be merciful, just as your Father also is merciful. Judge not, and you shall not be judged. Condemn not, and you shall not be condemned. Forgive, and you will be forgiven. Give, and it will be given to you: good measure, pressed down, shaken together, and running over will be put into your bosom. For with the same measure that you use, it will be measured back to you.

[27-C]   Take nothing for the journey, neither staffs nor bag nor bread nor money; and do not have two tunics apiece. Whatever house you enter, stay there, and from there depart. And whoever will not receive you, when you go out of that city, shake off the very dust from your feet as a testimony against them.

[28-C]   If anyone desires to come after Me, let him deny himself, and take up his cross daily, and follow Me.

[29-C]   Go your way; behold, I send you out as lambs among wolves. Carry neither money bag, knapsack, nor sandals; and greet no one along the road. But whatever house you enter, first say, 'Peace to this house.' And if a son of peace is there, your peace will rest on it; if not, it will return to you.

[30-C]   You have answered rightly; do this and you will live.

[31-C]   Sell what you have and give alms; provide yourselves money bags which do not grow old, a treasure in the heavens that does not fail, where no thief approaches nor moth destroys. For where your treasure is, there your heart will be also.

[32–C]   When you give a dinner or a supper, do not ask your friends, your brothers, your relatives, nor rich neighbors, lest they also invite you back, and you be repaid. But when you give a feast, invite the poor, the maimed, the lame, the blind. And you will be blessed, because they cannot repay you; for you shall be repaid at the resurrection of the just.

[33–C]   Take heed to yourselves. If your brother sins against you, rebuke him; and if he repents, forgive him. And if he sins against you seven times in a day, and seven times in a day returns to you, saying, 'I repent,' you shall forgive him.

[34–C]   *So Jesus said to him,* Why do you call Me good? No one is good but One, that is, God. You know the commandments: 'Do not commit adultery,' 'Do not murder,' 'Do not steal,' 'Do not bear false witness,' 'Honor your father and your mother.'

[35–C]   Watch therefore, and pray always that you may be counted worthy to escape all these things that will come to pass, and to stand before the Son of Man.

[36–C]   The kings of the Gentiles exercise lordship over them; and those who exercise authority over them are called 'benefactors.' But not so among you; on the contrary, he who is greatest among you, let him be as the younger, and he who governs as he who serves.

[37–D]   Do not labor for the food which perishes, but for the food which endures to eternal life, which the Son of man will give to you; for on him has God the Father set his seal.

[38–D]   Do not judge by appearances, but judge with right judgment.

[39–D]   While you have the light, believe in the light, that you may become sons of light. *When Jesus had said this, he departed and hid himself from them.*

[40–D]   A new commandment I give to you, that you love one another; even as I have loved you, that you also love one another.

[41–D]   This is my commandment, that you love one another as I have loved you.

[42–D]   This I command you, to love one another.

[43–F]   *His disciples questioned him and said to him, 'Do You want us to fast? How shall we pray? Shall we give alms? What diet shall we observe?'*
    Jesus said, Do not tell lies, and do not do what you hate, for all things are plain in the sight of Heaven. For nothing hidden will not become manifest, and nothing covered will remain without being uncovered.

[44–F]   *The disciples said to Jesus, 'We know that you will depart from us. Who will be our leader?'*
    Jesus said to them, Wherever you are, you are to go to James the righteous, for whose sake heaven and earth came into being.

[45–F]   *Jesus said,* When you see one who was not born of woman, prostrate yourselves on your faces and worship him. That one is your Father.

[46–F]   *Jesus said,* Love your brother like your soul, guard him like the pupil of your eye.

[47–F] *Jesus said,* Do not be concerned from morning until evening and from evening until morning about what you will wear.

[48–F] *Jesus said,* If you have money, do not lend it at interest, but give it to one from whom you will not get it back.

[49–G] Hasten to be saved without being urged! Instead, be eager of your own accord and, if possible, arrive even before me, for thus the Father will love you.

[50–G] Hearken to the word; understand knowledge; love life, and no one will persecute you, nor will any one oppress you, other than you yourselves.

[51–G] Do not make the kingdom of heaven a desert within you. Do not be proud because of the light that illumines, but be to yourselves as I myself am to you. For your sakes I have placed myself under the curse, that you may be saved.

[52–Q] And you therefore celebrate the remembrance of my death, i.e. the passover . . .

[53–Q] But look, a new commandment I give you, that you love one another and obey each other and that continual peace reign among you. Love your enemies, and what you do not want done to you, that do to no one else.

And both preach and teach this to those who believe in me, and preach concerning the kingdom of my Father, and as my Father has given me the power (so I give it to you) that you may bring near the children of the heavenly Father. Preach, and they will believe. You it is whose duty is to lead his children into heaven.

[54-Q]   Truly I say to you, preach and teach, as I will be with you. For I am well pleased to be with you, that you may become joint heirs with me of the kingdom of heaven of him who sent me.

[55-Q]   Go and preach to the twelve tribes of Israel and to the Gentiles and Israel and to the land of Israel towards East and West, North and South; and many will believe in me, the son of God.

[56-Q]   Go and preach and teach concerning the coming and the mercy of my Father.

[57-Q]   *And he said to us,* Go and preach and be good ministers and servants.

[58-Q]   But you, as you go, preach and teach truly and rightly, respecting and fearing the person of no one, but especially not that of the rich, among whom something will be found, who do not do my commandment, who revel in their riches. *And we said to him, 'O Lord, do you speak to us only of the rich?' And he said to us,* Also of him who is not rich; as soon as he gives and does not deny to him who has nothing, of such a one I say this: he will be called by men a doer.

[59-Q]   . . . Go in Peace.

[60-U]   Spread thou my gospel throughout the whole world in peace! For there will be rejoicing at the source of my word, the hope of life, and suddenly the world will be carried off.

[61-V]   He who has married should not repudiate his wife, and he who has not married should not marry.

II

Parables

[1–A]   But to what shall I liken this generation? It is like children sitting in the marketplaces and calling to their companions, and saying:
   'We played the flute for you,
   And you did not dance;
   We mourned to you,
   And you did not lament.'

[2–A]   *Then he spoke many things to them in parables, saying*: Behold, a sower went out to sow. And as he sowed, some seed fell by the wayside: and the birds came and devoured them. Some fell on stony places, where they did not have much earth; and they immediately sprang up because they had no depth of earth. But when the sun was up they were scorched, and because they had no root they withered away. And some fell among thorns, and the thorns sprang up and choked them. But others fell on good ground and yielded a crop: some a hundredfold, some sixty, some thirty. He who has ears to hear, let him hear!

[3-A]   For whoever has, to him more will be given, and he will have abundance; but whoever does not have, even what he has will be taken away from him.

[4-A]   When anyone hears the word of the kingdom, and does not understand it, then the wicked one comes and snatches away what was sown in his heart. This is he who received seed by the wayside. But he who received the seed on stony places, this is he who hears the word and immediately receives it with joy; yet he has no root in himself, but endures only for a while. For when tribulation or persecution arises because of the word, immediately he stumbles. Now he who received seed among the thorns is he who hears the word, and the cares of this world and the deceitfulness of riches choke the word, and he becomes unfruitful. But he who received seed on the good ground is he who hears the word and understands it, who indeed bears fruit and produces: some a hundredfold, some sixty, some thirty.

[5-A]   *Another parable He put forth to them, saying*: The kingdom of heaven is like a man who sowed good seed in his field; but while men slept, his enemy came and sowed tares among the wheat and went his way. But when the grain had sprouted and produced a crop, then the tares also appeared. So the servants of the owner came and said to him, 'Sir, did you not sow good seed in your field? How then does it have tares?'

He said to them, 'An enemy has done this.' The servants said to him, 'Do you want us then to go and gather them up?'

But he said, 'No, lest while you gather up the tares you also uproot the wheat with them. Let both grow together until the harvest, and at the time of harvest I will say to the reapers, "First gather together the tares and bind them in bundles to burn them, but gather the wheat into my barn."'

[6-A] *Another parable He put forth to them, saying,* The kingdom of heaven is like a mustard seed, which a man took and sowed in his field, which indeed is the least of all the seeds; but when it is grown it is greater than the herbs and becomes a tree, so that the birds of the air come and nest in its branches.

[7-A] *Another parable He spoke to them:* The kingdom of heaven is like leaven, which a woman took and hid in three measures of meal till it was all leavened.

[8-A] *He answered and said to them,* He who sows the good seed is the Son of Man. The field is the world, the good seeds are the sons of the kingdom, but the tares are the sons of the wicked one. The enemy who sowed them is the devil, the harvest is the end of the age, and the reapers are the angels. Therefore as the tares are gathered and burned in the fire, so it will be at the end of this age. The Son of Man will send out His angels, and they will gather out of His kingdom all things that offend, and those who practice lawlessness, and will cast them into the furnace of fire. There will be wailing and gnashing of teeth. Then the righteous will shine forth as the sun in the kingdom of their Father. He who has ears to hear, let him hear!

[9-A] Again, the kingdom of heaven is like treasure hidden in a field, which a man found and hid; and for joy over it he goes and sells all that he has and buys that field.

[10-A] Again, the kingdom of heaven is like a merchant seeking beautiful pearls, who, when he had found one pearl of great price, went and sold all that he had and bought it.

[11-A] Again, the kingdom of heaven is like a dragnet that was cast into the sea and gathered some of every kind, which, when it was full, they drew to shore; and they sat down and gathered the good into vessels, but threw the bad away. So it will be at the end of the age. The angels will come forth, separate the wicked from among the just, and cast them into the furnace of fire. There will be wailing and gnashing of teeth.

[12–A] *Then He said to them,* Therefore every scribe instructed concerning the kingdom of heaven is like a householder who brings out of his treasure things new and old.

[13–A] Every plant which My heavenly Father has not planted will be uprooted. Let them alone. They are blind leaders of the blind. And if the blind leads the blind, both will fall into a ditch.

[14–A] Do you not yet understand that whatever enters the mouth goes into the stomach and is eliminated?

[15–A] What do you think? If a man has a hundred sheep, and one of them goes astray, does he not leave the ninety-nine and go to the mountains to seek the one that is straying? And if he should find it, assuredly, I say to you, he rejoices more over that sheep than over the ninety-nine that did not go astray. Even so it is not the will of your Father who is in heaven that one of these little ones should perish.

[16–A] Therefore the kindom of heaven is like a certain king who wanted to settle accounts with his servants. And when he had begun to settle accounts, one was brought to him who owed him ten thousand talents. But as he was not able to pay, his master commanded that he be sold, with his wife and children and all that he had, and that payment be made. The servant therefore fell down before him, saying, 'Master, have patience with me, and I will pay you all.'

Then the master of that servant was moved with compassion, released him, and forgave him the debt. But that servant went out and found one of his fellow servants who owed him a hundred denarii; and he laid hands on him and took him by the throat, saying, 'Pay me what you owe!' So his fellow servant fell down at his feet and begged him, saying, 'Have patience with me, and I will pay you all.' And he would not, but went and threw him into prison till he should pay the debt.

So when his fellow servants saw what had been done, they were very grieved, and came and told their master all that had been done. Then his master, after he had called him, said to him, 'You wicked servant! I forgave you all that debt because you begged me. Should you not also have had compassion on your fellow servant, just as I had pity on you?' And his master was angry, and delivered him to the torturers until he should pay all that was due to him. So My heavenly Father also will do to you if each of you, from his heart, does not forgive his brother his trespasses.

[17–A] *Then said Jesus to His disciples,* Assuredly, I say to you that it is hard for a rich man to enter the kingdom of heaven. And again I say to you, it is easier for a camel to go through the eye of a needle than for a rich man to enter the kingdom of God.

[18–A] For the kingdom of heaven is like a landowner who went out early in the morning to hire laborers for his vineyard. Now when he had agreed with the laborers for a denarius a day, he sent them into his vineyard. And he went out about the third hour and saw others standing idle in the marketplace, and said to them, 'You also go into the vineyard, and whatever is right I will give you.' So they went. Again he went out about the sixth and the ninth hour, and did likewise. And about the eleventh hour he went out and found others standing idle, and said to them, 'Why have you been standing here idle all day?' They said to him, 'Because no one hired us.' He said to them, 'You also go into the vineyard, and whatever is right you will receive.'

So when evening had come, the owner of the vineyard said to his steward, 'Call the laborers and give them their wages, beginning with the last to the first.' And when those came who were hired about the eleventh hour, they each received a denarius. But when the first came, they supposed that they would receive more; and they likewise each received a denarius. And when they had received it, they complained against the landowner, saying, 'These last men have worked only one hour, and you made them equal to us who have borne the burden and the heat of the day.' But he answered one of them and said, 'Friend, I am doing you no wrong. Did you not agree with me for a denarius? Take what is yours and go your way. I wish to give to this last man the same as to you. Is it not lawful for me to do what I wish with my own things? Or is your eye evil because I am good?' So the last will be first, and the first last. For many are called, but few chosen.

[19–A]   But what do you think? A man had two sons, and he came to the first and said, 'Son, go, work today in my vineyard.' He answered and said, 'I will not,' but afterward he regretted it and went. Then he came to the second and said likewise. And he answered and said, 'I go, sir,' but he did not go. Which of the two did the will of his father? *They said to him, 'The first.' Jesus said to them*, Assuredly, I say to you that tax collectors and harlots enter the kingdom of God before you.

[20–A]   Hear another parable: There was a certain landowner who planted a vineyard and set a hedge around it, dug a winepress in it and built a tower. And he leased it to vinedressers and went into a far country. Now when vintage-time drew near, he sent his servants to the vinedressers, that they might receive its fruit. And the vine-dressers took his servants, beat one, killed one, and stoned another. Again he sent other servants, more than the first, and they did like-wise to them. Then last of all he sent his son to them, saying, 'They will respect my son.' But when the vinedressers saw the son, they said among themselves, 'This is the heir. Come, let us kill him and seize his inheritance.' So they took him and cast him out of the vineyard and killed him. Therefore, when the owner of the vineyard comes, what will he do to those vinedressers? *They said to Him, 'He will destroy those wicked men miserably, and lease his vineyard to other vinedressers who will render to him the fruits in their seasons.'*

[21–A]   *Jesus said to them,* Have you never read in the Scriptures:
'The stone which the builders rejected
Has become the chief cornerstone.
This was the Lord's doing
And it is marvelous in our eyes'?
Therefore I say to you, the kingdom of God will be taken from you and given to a nation bearing the fruits of it. And whoever falls on this stone will be broken; but on whomever it falls, it will grind him to powder.

[22–A]   The kingdom of heaven is like a certain king who arranged a marriage for his son, and sent out his servants to call those who were invited to the wedding; and they were not willing to come. Again, he sent out other servants, saying, 'Tell those who are in-vited, "See, I have prepared my dinner; my oxen and fatted cattle are killed, and all things are ready. Come to the wedding."

But they made light of it and went their ways, one to his own farm, another to his business. And the rest seized his servants, treated them spitefully, and killed them. But when the king heard about it, he was furious. And he sent out his armies, destroyed those murderers, and burned up their city. Then he said to his servants, 'The wedding is ready, but those who were invited were not worthy. Therefore go into the highways, and as many as you find, invite to the wedding.' So those servants went out into the highways and gathered together all whom they found, both bad and good. And the wedding hall was filled with guests.

[23–A]   But when the king came in to see the guests, he saw a man there who did not have on a wedding garment. So he said to him, 'Friend, how did you come in here without a wedding garment?' And he was speechless.

Then the king said to the servants, 'Bind him hand and foot, take him away, and cast him into outer darkness; there will be weeping and gnashing of teeth.' For many are called, but few are chosen.

[24–A]   Now learn this parable from the fig tree: When its branch has already become tender and puts forth leaves, you know that summer is near. So you also, when you see all these things, know that it is near — at the doors! Assuredly, I say to you, this generation will by no means pass away till all these things take place. Heaven and earth will pass away, but My words will by no means pass away.

[25–A]   Then the kingdom of heaven shall be likened to ten virgins who took their lamps and went out to meet the bridegroom. Now five of them were wise, and five were foolish. Those who were foolish took their lamps and took no oil with them, but the wise took oil in their vessels with their lamps. But while the bridegroom was delayed, they all slumbered and slept.

And at midnight a cry was heard: 'Behold, the bridegroom is coming; go out to meet him!' Then all those virgins arose and trimmed their lamps. And the foolish said to the wise, 'Give us some of your oil, for our lamps are going out.' But the wise answered, saying, 'No, lest there should not be enough for us and you; but go rather to those who sell, and buy for yourselves.'

And while they went to buy, the bridegroom came, and those who were ready went in with him to the wedding; and the door was shut. Afterward the other virgins came also, saying, 'Lord, Lord, open to us!' But he answered and said, 'Assuredly, I say to you, I do not know you.' Watch therefore, for you know neither the day nor the hour in which the Son of Man is coming.

[26-A]   For the Kingdom of heaven is like a man traveling to a far country, who called his own servants and delivered his goods to them. And to one he gave five talents, to another two, and to another one, to each according to his own ability; and immediately he went on a journey. Then he who had recieved the five talents went and traded with them, and made another five talents. And likewise he who had received two gained two more also. But he who had received one went and dug in the ground, and hid his lord's money.

After a long time the lord of those servants came and settled accounts with them. So he who had received five talents came and brought five other talents, saying, 'Lord, you delivered to me five talents; look, I have gained five more talents besides them.' His lord said to him, 'Well done, good and faithful servant; you were faithful over a few things, I will make you ruler over many things. Enter into the joy of your lord.'

He also who had received two talents came and said, 'Lord, you delivered to me two talents; look, I have gained two more talents besides them.' His lord said to him, 'Well done, good and faithful servant; you have been faithful over a few things, I will make you ruler over many things. Enter into the joy of your lord.'

Then he who had received the one talent came and said, 'Lord, I knew you to be a hard man, reaping where you have not sown, and gathering where you have not scattered seed. And I was afraid, and went and hid your talent in the ground. Look, there you have what is yours.'

But his lord answered and said to him, 'You wicked and lazy servant, you know that I reap where I have not sown, and gather where I have not scattered seed. So you ought to have deposited my money with the bankers, and at my coming I would have received back my own with interest. Therefore take the talent from him, and give it to him who has ten talents. For to everyone who has, more will be given, and he will have abundance; but from him who does not have, even what he has will be taken away. And cast the unprofitable servant into the outer darkness. There will be weeping and gnashing of teeth.'

[27–B]   Listen! A sower went out to sow. And as he sowed, some seed fell along the path, and the birds came and devoured it. Other seed fell on rocky ground, where it had not much soil, and immediately it sprang up, since it had no depth of soil; and when the sun rose it was scorched, and since it had no root it withered away. Other seed fell among thorns and the thorns grew up and choked it, and it yielded no grain. And other seeds fell into good soil and brought forth grain, growing up and increasing and yielding thirtyfold and sixtyfold and a hundredfold. *And he said*, He who has ears to hear, let him hear.

[28–B]   The sower sows the word. And these are the ones along the path, where the word is sown; when they hear, Satan immediately comes and takes away the word which is sown in them. And these in like manner are the ones sown upon rocky ground, who, when they hear the word, immediately receive it with joy; and they have no root in themselves, but endure for a while; then, when tribulation or persecution arises on account of the word, immediately they fall away. And others are the ones sown among thorns; they are those who hear the word, but the cares of the world, and the delight in riches, and the desire for other things, enter in and choke the word, and it proves unfruitful. But those that were sown upon the good soil are the ones who hear the word and accept it and bear fruit, thirtyfold and sixtyfold and a hundredfold.

[29-B]   *And he said to them,* Is a lamp brought in to be put under a bushel, or under a bed, and not on a stand? For there is nothing hid, except to be made manifest; nor is anything secret, except to come to light. If any man has ears to hear, let him hear.

[30-B]   For to him who has will more be given; and from him that has not, even what he has will be taken away.

[31-B]   *And he said,* The kingdom of God is as if a man should scatter seed upon the ground, and should sleep and rise night and day, and the seed should sprout and grow, he knows not how. The earth produces of itself, first the blade, then the ear, then the full grain in the ear. But when the grain is ripe, at once he puts in the sickle, because the harvest has come.

[32-B]   *And he said,* With what can we compare the kingdom of God, or what parable shall we use for it? It is like a grain of mustard seed, which, when sown upon the ground, is the smallest of all the seeds on earth; yet when it is sown it grows up and becomes the greatest of all shrubs, and puts forth large branches, so that the birds of the air can make nests in its shade.

[33-B]   Children, how hard it is to enter the kingdom of God! It is easier for a camel to go through the eye of a needle than for a rich man to enter the kingdom of God.

[34–B]   From the fig tree learn its lesson: as soon as its branch becomes tender and puts forth its leaves, you know that summer is near. So also, when you see these things taking place, you know that he is near, at the very gates. Truly, I say to you, this generation will not pass away before all these things take place. Heaven and earth will pass away, but my words will not pass away.

[35–C]   No one puts a piece from a new garment on an old one; otherwise the new makes a tear, and also the piece that was taken out of the new does not match the old. And no one puts new wine into old wineskins; or else the new wine will burst the wineskins and be spilled, and the wineskins will be ruined. But new wine must be put into new wineskins, and both are preserved. And no one, having drunk old wine, immediately desires new; for he says, 'The old is better.'

[36–C]   *And He spoke a parable to them*: Can the blind lead the blind? Will they not both fall into the ditch? A disciple is not above his teacher, but everyone who is perfectly trained will be like his teacher.

[37–C]   And why do you look at the speck in your brother's eye, but do not perceive the plank in your own eye? Or how can you say to your brother, 'Brother, let me remove the speck that is in your eye,' when you yourself do not see the plank that is in your own eye? Hypocrite! First remove the plank from your own eye, and then you will see clearly to remove the speck that is in your brother's eye.

[38–C]   For a good tree does not bear bad fruit, nor does a bad tree bear good fruit. For every tree is known by its own fruit. For men do not gather figs from thorns, nor do they gather grapes from a bramble bush. A good man out of the good treasure of his heart brings forth good; and an evil man out of the evil treasure of his heart brings forth evil. For out of the abundance of the heart his mouth speaks.

[39-C]   But why do you call Me 'Lord, Lord,' and not do the things which I say? Whoever comes to Me, and hears My sayings and does them, I will show you whom he is like: He is like a man building a house, who dug deep and laid the foundation on the rock. And when the flood arose, the stream beat vehemently against that house, and could not shake it, for it was founded on the rock. But he who heard and did nothing is like a man who built a house on the earth without a foundation, against which the stream beat vehemently; and immediately it fell. And the ruin of that house was great.

[40-C]   *And the Lord said,* To what then shall I liken the men of this generation, and what are they like? They are like children sitting in the marketplace and calling to one another, saying:
 'We played the flute for you,
 And you did not dance;
 We mourned to you,
 And you did not weep.'

[41-C]   There was a certain creditor who had two debtors. One owed five hundred denarii, and the other fifty. And when they had nothing with which to repay, he freely forgave them both. Tell Me, therefore, which of them will love him more? *Simon answered and said, 'I suppose the one whom he forgave more.' And He said to him,* You have rightly judged.

[42-C]   *But Jesus said to him,* No one, having put his hand to the plow, and looking back, is fit for the kingdom of God.

[43–C] A certain man went down from Jerusalem to Jericho, and fell among thieves, who stripped him of his clothing, wounded him, and departed, leaving him half dead. Now by chance a certain priest came down that road. And when he saw him, he passed by on the other side. Likewise a Levite, when he arrived at the place, came and looked, and passed by on the other side.

But a certain Samaritan, as he journeyed, came where he was. And when he saw him, he had compassion. So he went to him and bandaged his wounds, pouring on oil and wine; and he set him on his own animal, brought him to an inn, and took care of him. On the next day, when he departed, he took out two denarii, gave them to the innkeeper, and said to him, 'Take care of him; and whatever more you spend, when I come again, I will repay you.' So which of these three do you think was neighbor to him who fell among the thieves? *And he said, 'He who showed mercy on him.' Then Jesus said to him,* Go and do likewise.

[44–C] Which of you shall have a friend, and go to him at midnight and say to him, 'Friend, lend me three loaves; for a friend of mine has come to me on his journey, and I have nothing to set before him'; and he will answer from within and say, 'Do not trouble me; the door is now shut, and my children are with me in bed; I cannot rise and give to you'? I say to you, though he will not rise and give to him because he is his friend, yet because of his persistence he will rise and give him as many as he needs.

[45–C] No one, when he has lit a lamp, puts it in a secret place or under a basket, but on a lampstand, that those who come in may see the light. The lamp of the body is the eye. Therefore, when your eye is good, your whole body also is full of light. But when your eye is bad, your body also is full of darkness. Therefore take heed that the light which is in you is not darkness. If then your whole body is full of light, having no part dark, the whole body will be full of light, as when the bright shining of a lamp gives you light.

[46–C]   *Then he spoke a parable to them, saying*: The ground of a certain rich man yielded plentifully. And he thought within himself, saying, 'What shall I do, since I have no room to store my crops?' So he said, 'I will do this: I will pull down my barns and build greater, and there I will store all my crops and my goods. And I will say to my soul, "Soul, you have many goods laid up for many years; take your ease; eat, drink, and be merry."' But God said to him, 'Fool! This night your soul will be required of you; then whose will those things be which you have provided?' So is he who lays up treasure for himself, and is not rich toward God.

[47–C]   *And the Lord said*, Who then is that faithful and wise steward, whom his master will make ruler over his household, to give them their portion of food in due season? Blessed is that servant whom his master will find so doing when he comes. Truly, I say to you that he will make him ruler over all that he has.

But if that servant says in his heart, 'My master is delaying his coming,' and begins to beat the male and female servants, and to eat and drink and be drunk, the master of that servant will come on a day when he is not looking for him, and at an hour when he is not aware, and will cut him in two and appoint him his portion with the unbelievers. And that servant who knew his master's will, and did not prepare himself or do according to his will, shall be beaten with many stripes. But he who did not know, yet committed things deserving of stripes, shall be beaten with few. For everyone to whom much is given, from him much will be required; and to whom much has been committed, of him they will ask the more.

[48-C]   *He also spoke this parable*: A certain man had a fig tree planted in his vineyard, and he came seeking fruit on it and found none. Then he said to the keeper of his vineyard, 'Look, for three years I have come seeking fruit on this fig tree and find none. Cut it down; why does it use up the ground?' But he answered and said to him, 'Sir, let it alone this year also, until I dig around it and fertilize it. And if it bears fruit, well. But if not, after that you can cut it down.'

[49-C]   Strive to enter through the narrow gate, for many, I say to you, will seek to enter and will not be able. When once the Master of the house has risen up and shut the door, and you begin to stand outside and knock at the door, saying, 'Lord, Lord, open for us,' and He will answer and say to you, 'I do not know you, where you are from,' then you will begin to say, 'We ate and drank in Your presence, and You taught in our streets.' But He will say, 'I tell you I do not know you, where you are from. Depart from Me, all you workers of iniquity.'

There will be weeping and gnashing of teeth, when you see Abraham and Isaac and Jacob and all the prophets in the kingdom of God, and yourselves thrust out. They will come from the east and the west, from the north and the south, and sit down in the kingdom of God. And indeed there are last who will be first, and there are first who will be last.

[50-C]   When you are invited by anyone to a wedding feast, do not sit down in the best place, lest one more honorable than you be invited by him; and he who invited you and him come and say to you, 'Give place to this man,' and then you begin with shame to take the lowest place. But when you are invited, go and sit down in the lowest place, so that when he who invited you comes he may say to you, 'Friend, go up higher.' Then you will have glory in the presence of those who sit at the table with you. For whoever exalts himself will be humbled, and he who humbles himself will be exalted.

[51–C]   A certain man made a great supper and invited many, and sent his servant at supper time to say to those that were invited, 'Come, for all things are now ready.' But they all with one accord began to make excuses. The first said to him, 'I have bought a piece of ground, and I must go and see it. I ask you to have me excused.' And another said, 'I have bought five yoke of oxen, and I go to test them. I ask you to have me excused.' Still another said, 'I have married a wife, therefore I cannot come.'

So that servant came and reported these things to his master. Then the master of the house, being angry, said to his servant, 'Go out quickly into the streets and lanes of the city, and bring in here the poor and the maimed and the lame and the blind.' And the servant said, 'Master, it is done as you commanded, and still there is room.' Then the master said to the servant, 'Go out into the highways and hedges, and compel them to come in, that my house may be filled. For I say to you that none of those men who were invited shall taste my supper.'

[52–C]   For which of you, intending to build a tower, does not sit down first and count the cost, whether he has enough to finish it — lest, after he has laid the foundation, and is not able to finish, all who see it begin to mock him, saying, 'This man began to build and was not able to finish.'

[53–C]   Or what king, going to make war against another king, does not sit down first and consider whether he is able with ten thousand to meet him who comes against him with twenty thousand? Or else, while the other is still a great way off, he sends a delegation and asks conditions of peace. So likewise, whoever of you does not forsake all that he has cannot be My disciple.

[54-C]   Salt is good; but if the salt has lost its flavor, how shall it be seasoned? It is neither fit for the land nor for the dunghill, but men throw it out. He who has ears to hear, let him hear!

[55-C]   What man of you, having a hundred sheep, if he loses one of them, does not leave the ninety-nine in the wilderness, and go after the one which is lost until he finds it? And when he has found it, he lays it on his shoulders, rejoicing. And when he comes home, he calls together his friends and neighbors, saying to them, 'Rejoice with me, for I have found my sheep which was lost!' I say to you that likewise there will be more joy in heaven over one sinner who repents than over ninety-nine just persons who need no repentance.

[56-C]   Or what woman, having ten silver coins, if she loses one coin, does not light a lamp, sweep the house, and search carefully until she finds it? And when she has found it, she calls her friends and neighbors together, saying, 'Rejoice with me, for I have found the piece which I lost!' Likewise, I say to you, there is joy in the presence of the angels of God over one sinner who repents.

[57-C]   A certain man had two sons. And the younger of them said to his father, 'Father, give me the portion of goods that falls to me.' So he divided to them his livelihood. And not many days after, the younger son gathered all together, journeyed to a far country, and there wasted his possessions with prodigal living. But when he had spent all, there arose a severe famine in that land, and he began to be in want. Then he went and joined himself to a citizen of that country, and he sent him into his fields to feed swine. And he would gladly have filled his stomach with the pods that the swine ate, and no one gave him anything. But when he came to himself, he said, 'How many of my father's hired servants have bread enough and to spare, and I perish with hunger! I will arise and go to my father, and will say to him, Father, I have sinned against heaven and before you, and I am no longer worthy to be called your son. Make me like one of your hired servants.'

And he arose and came to his father. But when he was still a great way off, his father saw him and had compassion, and ran and fell on his neck and kissed him. And the son said to him, 'Father, I have sinned against heaven and in your sight, and am no longer worthy to be called your son.' But the father said to his servants, 'Bring out the best robe and put it on him, and put a ring on his hand and sandals on his feet. And bring the fatted calf here and kill it, and let us eat and be merry; for this my son was dead and is alive again; he was lost and is found.' And they began to be merry.

Now his older son was in the field. And as he came and drew near to the house, he heard music and dancing. So he called one of the servants and asked what these things meant. And he said to him, 'Your brother has come, and because he has received him safe and sound, your father has killed the fatted calf.' But he was angry and would not go in. Therefore his father came out and pleaded with him. So he answered and said to his father, 'Lo, these many years I have been serving you; I never transgressed your commandment at any time; and yet you never gave me a young goat, that I might make merry with my friends. But as soon as this son of yours came, who has devoured your livelihood with harlots, you killed the fatted calf for him.'

And he said to him, 'Son, you are always with me, and all that I have is yours. It was right that we should make merry and be glad, for your brother was dead and is alive again, and was lost and is found.'

[58-C] *He also said to his disciples:* There was a certain rich man who had a steward, and an accusation was brought to him that this man was wasting his goods. So he called him and said to him, 'What is this I hear about you? Give an account of your stewardship, for you can no longer be steward.' Then the steward said within himself, 'What shall I do? For my master is taking the stewardship away from me. I cannot dig; I am ashamed to beg. I have resolved what to do, that when I am put out of the stewardship, they may receive me into their houses.'

So he called every one of his master's debtors to him, and said to the first, 'How much do you owe my master?' And he said, 'A hundred measures of oil.' So he said to him, 'Take your bill, and sit down quickly and write fifty.' Then he said to another, 'And how much do you owe?' So he said, 'A hundred measures of wheat.' And he said to him, 'Take your bill, and write eighty.' So the master commended the unjust steward because he had dealt shrewdly. For the sons of this world are more shrewd in their generation than the sons of light.

[59–C] No servant can serve two masters; for either he will hate the one and love the other; or else he will be loyal to the one and despise the other. You cannot serve God and mammon.

[60–C] There was a certain rich man who was clothed in purple and fine linen and fared sumptuously every day. But there was a certain beggar named Lazarus, full of sores, who was laid at his gate, desiring to be fed with the crumbs which fell from the rich man's table. Moreover the dogs came and licked his sores. So it was that the beggar died, and was carried by the angels to Abraham's bosom. The rich man also died and was buried. And being in torments in Hades, he lifted up his eyes and saw Abraham afar off, and Lazarus in his bosom. Then he cried and said, 'Father Abraham, have mercy on me, and send Lazarus that he may dip the tip of his finger in water and cool my tongue; for I am tormented in this flame.'

But Abraham said, 'Son, remember that in your lifetime you received your good things, and likewise Lazarus evil things; but now he is comforted and you are tormented. And besides all this, between us and you there is a great gulf fixed, so that those who want to pass from here to you cannot, nor can those from there pass to us.' Then he said, 'I beg you therefore, father, that you would send him to my father's house, for I have five brothers, that he may testify to them, lest they also come to this place of torment.' Abraham said to him, 'They have Moses and the prophets; let them hear them.' And he said, 'No, father Abraham; but if one goes to them from the dead, they will repent.' But he said to him, 'If they do not hear Moses and the prophets, neither will they be persuaded though one rise from the dead.'

[61–C]   And which of you, having a servant plowing or tending sheep, will say to him when he has come in from the field, 'Come at once and sit down to eat'? But will he not rather say to him, 'Prepare something for my supper, and gird yourself and serve me till I have eaten and drunk, and afterward you will eat and drink'? Does he thank that servant because he did the things that were commanded him? I think not. So likewise you, when you have done all those things which you are commanded, say, 'We are unprofitable servants. We have done what was our duty to do.'

[62–C]   There was in a certain city a judge who did not fear God nor regard man. Now there was a widow in that city; and she came to him, saying, 'Get justice for me from my adversary.' And he would not for a while; but afterward he said within himself, 'Though I do not fear God nor regard man, yet because this widow troubles me I will avenge her, lest by her continual coming she weary me.' *Then the Lord said*, Hear what the unjust judge said. And shall God not avenge His own elect who cry out day and night to

Him, though He bears long with them? I tell you that He will avenge them speedily. Nevertheless, when the Son of Man comes, will He find faith on the earth?

[63–C]   Two men went up to the temple to pray, one a Pharisee and the other a tax collector. The Pharisee stood and prayed thus with himself, 'God, I thank You that I am not like other men — extortioners, unjust, adulterers, or even as this tax collector. I fast twice a week; I give tithes of all that I possess.' And the tax collector, standing afar off, would not so much as raise his eyes to heaven, but beat his breast, saying, 'God, be merciful to me a sinner!' I tell you, this man went down to his house justified rather than the other; for everyone who exalts himself will be humbled, and he who humbles himself will be exalted.

[64–C]   A certain nobleman went into a far country to receive for himself a kingdom and to return. So he called ten of his servants, delivered to them ten minas, and said to them, 'Do business till I come.' But his citizens hated him, and sent a delegation after him, saying, 'We will not have this man to reign over us.'

And so it was that when he returned, having received the kingdom, he then commanded these servants, to whom he had given the money, to be called to him, that he might know how much every man had gained by trading. Then came the first, saying, 'Master, your mina has earned ten minas.' And he said to him, 'Well done, good servant; because you were faithful in a very little, have authority over ten cities.' And the second came, saying, 'Master, your mina has earned five minas.' Likewise he said to him, 'You also be over five cities.' Then another came, saying, 'Master, here is your mina, which I have kept put away in a handkerchief. For I feared you, because you are an austere man. You collect what you did not deposit, and reap what you did not sow.' And he said to him, 'Out of your own mouth I will judge you, you wicked servant. You knew that I was an austere man, collecting what I did not deposit and reaping what I did not sow. Why then did you not put my money in the bank, that at my coming I might have collected it with interest?'

And he said to those who stood by, 'Take the mina from him, and give it to him who has ten minas.' (But they said to him, 'Master, he has ten minas.') For I say to you, that to everyone who has will be given; and from him who does not have, even what he has will be taken away from him. But bring here those enemies of mine, who did not want me to reign over them, and slay them before me.'

[65–D]   Truly, truly, I say to you, he who does not enter the sheepfold by the door but climbs in by another way, that man is a thief and a robber; but he who enters by the door is the shepherd of the sheep. To him the gatekeeper opens; the sheep hear his voice, and he calls his own sheep by name and leads them out. When he has brought out all his own, he goes before them, and the sheep follow him, for they know his voice. A stranger they will not follow, but they will flee from him, for they do not know the voice of strangers.

[66–D]   Truly, truly, I say to you, I am the door of the sheep. All who came before me are thieves and robbers; but the sheep did not heed them. I am the door; if any one enters by me, he will be saved, and will go in and out and find pasture. The thief comes only to steal and kill and destroy; I came that they may have life, and have it abundantly. I am the good shepherd. The good shepherd lays down his life for the sheep.

[67–D]   He flees because he is a hireling and cares nothing for the sheep. I am the good shepherd; I know my own and my own know me, as the Father knows me and I know the Father; and I lay down my life for the sheep. And I have other sheep, that are not of this fold; I must bring them also, and they will heed my voice. So there shall be one flock, one shepherd. For this reason the Father loves me, because I lay down my life, that I may take it again. No one takes it from me, but I lay it down of my own accord. I have power to lay it down, and I have power to take it again; this charge I have received from my Father.

[68–D]   I am the true vine, and my Father is the vinedresser. Every branch of mine that bears not fruit, he takes away, and every branch that does bear fruit he prunes, that it may bear more fruit. You are already made clean by the word which I have spoken to you. Abide in me, and I in you. As the branch cannot bear fruit by itself, unless it abides in the vine, neither can you, unless you abide in me. I am the vine, you are the branches. He who abides in me, and I in him, he it is that bears much fruit, for apart from me you can do nothing. If a man does not abide in me, he is cast forth as a branch and withers; and the branches are gathered, thrown into the fire and burned.

[69–F]   *And he said,* The man is like a wise fisherman who cast his net into the sea and drew it up from the sea full of small fish. Among them the wise fisherman found a fine large fish. He threw all the small fish back into the sea and chose the large fish without difficulty. Whoever has ears to hear, let him hear.

[70–F]   *Jesus said,* Now the sower went out, took a handful of seeds, and scattered them. Some fell on the road; the birds came and gathered them up. Others fell on rock, did not take root in the soil, and did not produce ears. And others fell on thorns; they choked the seeds and worms ate them. And others fell on the good soil and produced good fruit: it bore sixty per measure and a hundred and twenty per measure.

[71-F]   *The disciples said to Jesus, 'Tell us what the kingdom of heaven is like.' He said to them,* It is like a mustard seed, the smallest of all seeds. But when it falls on tilled soil, it produces a great plant and becomes a shelter for birds of the sky.

[72-F]   *Mary said to Jesus, 'Whom are your disciples like?' He said,* They are like children who have settled in a field which is not theirs. When the owners of the field come, they will say, 'Let us have back our field.' They will undress in their presence in order to let them have back their field and to give it back to them. Therefore I say to you, if the owner of a house knows that the thief is coming, he will begin his vigil before he comes and will not let him dig through into his house of his domain to carry away his goods. You then, be on your guard against the world. Arm yourself with great strength lest the robbers find a way to come to you, for the difficulty which you expect will surely materialize. Let there be among you a man of understanding. When the grain ripened, he came quickly with his sickle in his hand and reaped it. Whoever has ears to hear, let him hear.

[73-F]   *Jesus said,* Preach from your housetops that which you will hear in your ear and in the other ear. For no one lights a lamp and puts it under a bushel, nor does he put it in a hidden place, but rather he sets it on a lampstand so that everyone who enters and leaves will see its light.

[74-F]   *Jesus said,* It is not possible for anyone to enter the house of a strong man and take it by force unless he binds his hands; then he will be able to ransack his house.

[75–F]   *Jesus said*, A grapevine has been planted outside of the Father, but being unsound, it will be pulled up by its roots and destroyed.

[76–F]   *Jesus said*, Grapes are not harvested from thorns, nor are figs gathered from thistles, for they do not produce fruit. A good man brings forth good from his storehouse; an evil man brings forth evil things from his evil storehouse, which is in his heart, and says evil things. For out of the abundance of the heart he brings forth evil things.

[77–F]   *Jesus said*, It is impossible for a man to mount two horses or to stretch two bows. And it is impossible for a servant to serve two masters; otherwise, he will honor the one and treat the other contemptuously. No man drinks old wine and immediately desires to drink new wine. And new wine is not put into old wineskins, lest they burst; nor is old wine put into a new wineskin, lest it spoil it. An old patch is not sewn onto a new garment, because a tear would result.

[78–F]   *Jesus said*, The Kingdom of the Father is like a man who had good seed. His enemy came by night and sowed weeds among the good seed. The man did not allow them to pull up the weeds; he said to them, 'I am afraid that you will go intending to pull up the weeds and pull up the wheat along with them.' For on the day of the harvest the weeds will be plainly visible, and they will be pulled up and burned.

[79–F]   *Jesus said*, There was a rich man who had much money. He said, 'I shall put my money to use so that I may sow, reap, plant, and fill my storehouse with produce, with the result that I shall lack nothing.' Such were his intentions, but that same night he died. Let him who has ears hear.

[80–F] *Jesus said*, A man had received visitors. And when he had prepared the dinner, he sent his servant to invite the guests. He went to the first one and said, 'My master invites you.' He said, 'I have claims against some merchants. They are coming to me this evening. I must go and give them my orders. I ask to be excused from the dinner.' He went to another and said to him, 'My master has invited you.' He said to him, 'I have just bought a house and am required for the day. I shall not have any spare time.' He went to another and said to him, 'My master invited you.' He said to him, 'My friend is going to get married, and I am to prepare the banquet. I shall not be able to come. I ask to be excused from the dinner.' He went to another and said to him, 'My master invites you.' He said to him, 'I have just bought a farm, and I am on my way to collect the rent. I shall not be able to come. I ask to be excused.' The servant returned and said to his master, 'Those whom you invited to the dinner have asked to be excused.' The master said to the servant, 'Go outside to the streets and bring back those whom you happen to meet, so that they may dine.' Businessmen and merchants will not enter the Places of My Father.

[81–F] *He said*, There was a good man who owned a vineyard. He leased it to tenant farmers so that they might work it and he might collect the produce from them. He sent his servant so that the tenants might give him the produce of the vineyard. They seized his servant and beat him, all but killing him. The servant went back and told his master. The master said, 'Perhaps they did not recognize him.' He sent another servant. The tenants beat this one as well. Then the owner sent his son and said, 'Perhaps they will show respect to my son.' Because the tenants knew that it was he who was the heir to the vineyard, they seized him and killed him. Let him who has ears hear.

[82–F]　*Jesus said*, Many are standing at the door, but it is the solitary who will enter the bridal chamber.

[83–F]　*Jesus said*, The Kingdom of the Father is like a merchant who had a consignment of merchandise and who discovered a pearl. That merchant was shrewd. He sold the merchandise and bought the pearl alone for himself. You too, seek his unfailing and enduring treasure where no moth comes near to devour and no worm destroys.

[84–F]　*Jesus said*, The Kingdom of the Father is like a certain woman. She took a little leaven, concealed it in some dough, and made it into large loaves. Let him who has ears hear.

[85–F]　*Jesus said*, The Kingdom of the Father is like a certain woman who was carrying a jar full of meal. While she was walking on a road, still some distance from home, the handle of the jar broke and the meal emptied out behind her on the road. She did not realize it; she had noticed no accident. When she reached her house, she set the jar down and found it empty.

[86–F]　*Jesus said*, The Kingdom of the Father is like a certain man who wanted to kill a powerful man. In his own house he drew his sword and stuck it into the wall in order to find out whether his hand could carry through. Then he slew the powerful man.

[87–F]　*Jesus said*, Fortunate is the man who knows where the brigands will enter, so that he may get up, muster his domain, and arm himself before they invade.

[88–F]　*Jesus said*, The Kingdom is like a shepherd who had a hundred sheep. One of them, the largest, went astray. He left the ninety-nine and looked for that one until he found it. When he had gone to such trouble, he said to the sheep, 'I care for you more than the ninety-nine.'

[89-F]   *Jesus said*, The Kingdom is like a man who had a hidden treasure in his field without knowing it. And after he died, he left it to his son. The son did not know about the treasure. He inherited the field and sold it. And the one who bought it went plowing and found the treasure. He began to lend money at interest to whomever he wished.

[90-G]   Do not allow the kingdom of heaven to wither; for it is like a palm shoot whose fruit has poured down around it. It put forth leaves, and after they had sprouted they caused the pith to dry up. So it is also with the fruit which has grown from this single root: when it had been picked, fruit was borne by many. It (the root) was certainly good, and if it were possible to produce the new plants now, you would find it.

[91-G]   Become earnest about the Word! For as to the Word, its first part is faith, the second, love, the third, works; for from these comes life. For the Word is like a grain of wheat: when someone had sown it, he had faith in it; and when it had sprouted, he loved it because he had seen many grains in place of one. And when he had worked, he was saved because he had prepared it for food, and again he left some to sow. So also can you yourselves receive the kingdom of heaven; unless you receive this through knowledge, you will not be able to find it.

[92-G]   For this cause I tell you this, that you may know yourselves. For the kingdom of heaven is like an ear of grain after it had sprouted in a field. And when it had ripened, it scattered its fruit

and again filled the field with ears for another year. You also: hasten
to reap an ear of life for youselves that you may be filled with the
kingdom!

[93-G]   And once more I prevail upon you, for I am revealed to
you building a house which is of great value to you since you find
shelter beneath it, just as it will be able to stand by your neighbors'
house when it threatens to fall.

[94-I]   The sun and the moon will give a fragrance to you, together with the air and the spirit and the earth and the water. For if
the sun does not shine upon these bodies, they will wither and perish just like weeds or grass. If the sun shines on the weeds, it prevails
and chokes the grapevine; but if the grapevine prevails and shades
those weeds and all that other brush growing alongside and spreads
and flourishes, it alone inherits the land in which it grows and dominates every place it shaded. And then when it grows up, it dominates
all the land and is bountiful for its master, and it pleases him even
more, for he would have suffered great pains on account of these
plants until he uprooted them. But the grapevine alone removed
them and choked them, and they died and became like the soil.

[95-J]   For people do not gather figs from thorns or from thorn
trees, if they are wise, nor grapes from thistles. For on the one hand,
that which is always becoming is in that from which it is, being from
what is not good, which becomes destruction for it (the soul) and
death. But that (immortal soul) which comes to be in the Eternal
One is in the One of the life and the immortality of the life which
they resemble.

[96-Q]   *And we said to him, 'O master, do we have together with them*
one hope of the inheritance?' He answered and said to us, Are the fingers

of the hand alike or the ears of corn in the field? Or do the fruit-bearing trees give the same fruit? Do they not bring forth fruit according to their nature?

[97-Q]   I say this to you that you may do as I have done to you; and be as the wise virgins who kindled the light and did not slumber and who went with their lamps to meet the lord, the bridegroom, and have gone in with him into the bridegroom's chamber. But the foolish ones who talked with them were not able to watch, but fell asleep. *And we said to him, 'O Lord, who are the wise and who the foolish?' And he said to us,* The wise are these five, who are called by the prophet daughters of God, whose names let men hear. *But we were sad and troubled and wept for those who had been shut out. And he said to us,* The five wise are these: Faith, Love, Joy, Peace, Hope. As soon as they who believe in me have these, they will be leaders to those who believe in me and in him who sent me. I am the Lord and I am the bridegroom; they have received me and have gone with me into the house of the bridegroom, and laid themselves down at table with the bridegroom and rejoiced. But the five foolish slept, and when they awoke they came to the house of the bridegroom and knocked at the doors, for they had been shut; and they wept, because they were shut.

[98-Q]   Whoever is shut out is shut out. *And we said to him, 'O Lord, is this thing definite? Who now are these foolish ones?' And he said to us,* Listen: Insight, Knowledge, Obedience, Endurance, Mercy. These have slept in those who have believed and acknowledged me. And since those who slept did not fulfill my commandment, they will be outside the kingdom and the fold of the shepherd; and whoever remains outside the fold will the wolf eat. And although he hears he will be judged and will die, and much suffering and distress and endurance will come upon him;

and although he is badly pained and although he is cut into pieces and lacerated with long and painful punishment, yet he will not be able to die quickly.

[99-U]   Dost thou not understand that the fig-tree is the house of Israel? Even as a man hath planted a fig-tree in his garden and it brought forth no fruit, and he sought its fruit for many years. When he found it not, he said to the keeper of his garden, 'Uproot the fig-tree that our land may not be unfruitful for us.' And the gardener said to God, 'We thy servants wish to clear it of weeds and to dig the ground around it and to water it. If it does not then bear fruit, we will immediately remove its roots from the garden and plant another one in its place.'

[100-U]   Behold and consider the corns of wheat which are sown in the earth. As something dry and without a soul does a man sow them in the earth; and they live again, bear fruit, and the earth gives them back again as a pledge entrusted to it. And this which dies, which is sown as seed in the earth and shall become alive and be restored to life, is man. How much more shall God raise up on the day of decision those who believe in him and are chosen by him and for whom he made the earth. And all this shall the earth give back on the day of decision, since it shall also be judged with them, and the heaven with it.

III

<hr>

Jesus Speaking about Himself

[1-A]   Do not think that I came to destroy the Law or the Prophets. I did not come to destroy but to fulfill.

[2-A]   *And Jesus said to him,* Foxes have holes and birds of the air have nests, but the Son of Man has nowhere to lay His head.

[3-A]   Can the friends of the bridegroom mourn as long as the bridegroom is with them? But the days will come when the bridegroom will be taken away from them, and then they will fast.

[4-A]   Yet I say to you that in this place there is One greater than the temple.

[5-A]   For the Son of Man is Lord even of the Sabbath.

[6–A]   A prophet is not without honor except in his own country and in his own house.

[7–A]   I was not sent except to the lost sheep of the house of Israel.

[8–A]   For where two or three are gathered together in My name, I am there in the midst of them.

[9–A]   Behold, we are going up to Jerusalem, and the Son of Man will be betrayed to the chief priests and to the scribes; and they will condemn Him to death . . .

[10–A]   . . . just as the Son of Man did not come to be served, but to serve, and to give His life a ransom for many.

[11–A]   *And as they were eating, Jesus took bread, blessed and broke it, and gave it to the disciples and said,* Take, eat; this is My body. *Then He took the cup, and gave thanks, and gave it to them, saying,* Drink from it, all of you. For this is My blood of the new covenant, which is shed for many for the remission of sins.

[12–A]   I am able to destroy the temple of God, and to build it in three days.

[13–A]   It is as you said. Nevertheless, I say to you, hereafter you will see the Son of Man sitting at the right hand of the power, and coming on the clouds of heaven.

[14–A]   *And Jesus came and spoke to them, saying,* All authority has been given to Me in heaven and on earth.

[15–B]   Those who are well have no need of a physician, but those who are sick; I came not to call the righteous, but sinners.

[16–B]   For the Son of man also came not to be served, but to serve, and to give his life as a ransom for many.

[17–B]   It is like a man going on a journey, when he leaves home and puts his servants in charge, each with his work, and commands the doorkeeper to be on the watch.

[18–C]   *But He said to them,* I must preach the kingdom of God to the other cities also, because for this purpose I have been sent.

[19–C]   The Son of Man must suffer many things, and be rejected by the elders and chief priests and scribes, and be killed, and be raised the third day.

[20–C]   Let these words sink down into your ears, for the Son of Man is about to be betrayed into the hands of men.

[21–C]   All things have been delivered to Me by My Father, and no one knows who the Son is except the Father; and who the Father is except the Son, and the one to whom the Son wills to reveal Him.

[22–C]   For who is greater, he who sits at the table, or he who serves? Is it not he who sits at the table? Yet I am among you as the One who serves.

[23–D]   Destroy this temple, and in three days I will raise it up.

[24–D]   And as Moses lifted up the serpent in the wilderness, so must the Son of man be lifted up, that whoever believes in him may have eternal life.

[25-D]   For God so loved the world that he gave his only Son, that whoever believes in him should not perish but have eternal life. For God sent the Son into the world, not to condemn the world, but that the world might be saved through him.

[26-D]   Truly, truly, I say to you, the Son can do nothing of his own accord, but only what he sees the Father doing; for whatever he does, that the Son does likewise. For the Father loves the Son, and shows him all that he himself is doing; and greater works than these will he show him, that you may marvel. For as the Father raises the dead and gives them life, so also the Son gives life to whom he will.

[27-D]   The Father judges no one, but has given all judgment to the Son, that all may honor the Son, even as they honor the Father. He who does not honor the Son does not honor the Father who sent him.

[28-D]   I can do nothing on my own authority; as I hear, I judge; and my judgment is just, because I seek not my own will but the will of him who sent me. If I bear witness to myself, my testimony is not true.

[29-D]   You search the scriptures, because you think that in them you have eternal life; and it is they that bear witness to me; yet you refuse to come to me that you may have life.

[30-D]   I do not receive glory from men. But I know that you have not the love of God within you. I have come in my Father's name, and you do not receive me; if another comes in his own name, him you will receive.

[31–D]   *Jesus said to them*, I am the bread of life; he who comes to me shall not hunger, and he who believes in me shall never thirst.

[32–D]   For I have come down from heaven, not to do my own will, but the will of him who sent me, and this is the will of him who sent me, that I should lose nothing of all that he has given me, but raise it up at the last day.

[33–D]   For this is the will of my Father, that every one who sees the Son and believes in him should have eternal life; and I will raise him up at the last day.

[34–D]   I am the bread of life.

[35–D]   I am the living bread which came down from heaven; if any one eats of this bread, he will live for ever; and the bread which I shall give for the life of the world is my flesh.

[36–D]   The world cannot hate you, but it hates me because I testify of it that its works are evil. Go to the feast yourselves; I am not going up to this feast, for my time has not yet fully come.

[37–D]   My teaching is not mine, but his who sent me.

[38–D]   You know me, and you know where I come from? But I have not come of my own accord; he who sent me is true, and him you do not know. I know him, for I come from him, and he sent me.

[39–D]   *Jesus then said*, I shall be with you a little longer, and then I go to him who sent me; you will seek me and you will not find me; where I am you cannot come.

[40-D] Even if I do bear witness to myself, my testimony is true, for I know whence I have come and whither I am going, but you do not know whence I come or whither I am going. You judge according to the flesh, I judge no one. Yet even if I do judge, my judgment is true, for it is not I alone that judge, but I and he who sent me.

[41-D] I bear witness to myself, and the Father who sent me bears witness to me.

[42-D] *He said to them*, You are from below, I am from above; you are of this world, I am not of this world.

[43-D] I have much to say about you and much to judge; but he who sent me is true, and I declare to the world what I have heard from him. *They did not understand that he spoke to them of the Father. So Jesus said*, When you have lifted up the Son of man, then you will know that I am he, and that I do nothing on my own authority but speak thus as the Father taught me. And he who sent me is with me; he has not left me alone, for I always do what is pleasing to him.

[44-D] I have not a demon; but I honor my Father, and you dishonor me. Yet I do not seek my own glory; there is One who seeks it and he will be the judge. Truly, truly, I say to you, if any one keeps my word, he will never see death.

[45-D] If I glorify myself, my glory is nothing; it is my Father who glorifies me, of whom you say that he is your God. But you have not known him; I know him. If I said, I do not know him, I should be a liar like you; but I do know him and I keep his word.

[46-D]   *Jesus said to them,* Truly, truly, I say to you, before Abraham was, I am.

[47-D]   We must work the works of him who sent me, while it is day; night comes, when no one can work. As long as I am in the world, I am the light of the world.

[48-D]   I told you, and you do not believe. The works that I do in my Father's name, they bear witness to me; but you do not believe, because you do not belong to my sheep.

[49-D]   My sheep hear my voice, and I know them, and they follow me; and I give them eternal life, and they shall never perish, and no one shall snatch them out of my hand. My Father, who has given them to me, is greater than all, and no one is able to snatch them out of the Father's hand.

[50-D]   I and the Father are one.

[51-D]   Truly, truly, I say to you, unless a grain of wheat falls into the earth and dies, it remains alone; but if it dies, it bears much fruit.

[52-D]   If any one serves me, he must follow me; and where I am, there shall my servant be also; if any one serves me, the Father will honor him. Now is my soul troubled. And what shall I say? 'Father, save me from this hour?'

[53-D]   And I, when I am lifted up from the earth, will draw all men to myself.

[54-D]   *Jesus cried out and said,* He who believes in me, believes not in me but in him who sent me. And he who sees me sees him who sent me. I have come as light into the world, that whoever believes in me may not remain in darkness. If any one hears my sayings and does not keep them, I do not judge him; for I did not come to judge the world but to save the world.

[55-D]   He who rejects me and does not receive my sayings has a judge; the word that I have spoken will be his judge on the last day.

[56-D]   You call me Teacher and Lord; and you are right, for so I am. If I then, your Lord and Teacher, have washed your feet, you also ought to wash one another's feet. For I have given you an example, that you also should do as I have done to you.

[57-D]   *Jesus said to him*, I am the way, and the truth, and the life; no one comes to the Father, but by me. If you had known me, you would have known my Father also; henceforth you know him, and have seen him.

[58-D]   If you ask anything in my name, I will do it. If you love me, you will keep my commandments.

[59-D]   Greater love has no man than this, that a man lay down his life for his friends.

[60-D]   All that the Father has is mine; therefore I said that he will take what is mine and declare it to you. A little while, and you will see me no more; again a little while, and you will see me.

[61-D]   And now I am no more in the world, but they are in the world, and I am coming to thee. Holy Father, keep them in my name, which thou hast given me, that they may be one, even as we are one. While I was with them, I kept them in thy name, which thou hast given me; I have guarded them, and none of them is lost but the son of perdition, that the scripture might be fulfilled. But now I am coming to thee; and these things I speak in the world, that they may have my joy fulfilled in themselves.

[62–D] I have spoken openly to the world; I have always taught in synagogues and in the temple, where all Jews come together; I have said nothing secretly.

[63–E] I am Alpha and Omega, the beginning and the ending, *saith the Lord*, which is, and which was, and which is to come, the Almighty.

[64–E] Fear not; I am the first and the last: I am he that liveth, and was dead: and behold, I am alive for evermore, A'-men; and have the keys of hell and of death.

[65–E] Behold, I come as a thief. Blessed is he that watcheth, and keepeth his garments, lest he walk naked, and they see his shame.

[66–F] *Jesus said*, I have cast fire upon the world, and see, I am guarding it until it blazes.

[67–F] *Jesus said to his disciples*, Compare me to someone and tell me whom I am like. *Simon Peter said to him, 'You are like a righteous angel.' Matthew said to him, 'You are like a wise philosopher.' Thomas said to him, 'Master, my mouth is wholly incapable of saying whom You are like.'*

Jesus said, I am not your master. Because you have drunk, you have become intoxicated from the bubbling spring which I have measured out.

[68–F]   *Jesus said,* Men think, perhaps, that it is peace which I have come to cast upon the world. They do not know that it is dissension which I have come to cast upon the earth: fire, sword, and war. For there will be five in a house: three will be against two, and two against three, the father against the son, and the son against the father. And they will stand solitary.

[69–F]   *Jesus said,* I shall give you what no eye has seen and what no ear has heard and what no hand has touched and what has never occurred to the human mind.

[70–F]   *Jesus said,* I took my place in the midst of the world, and I appeared to them in flesh. I found all of them intoxicated; I found none of them thirsty. And My soul became afflicted for the sons of men, because they are blind in their hearts and do not have sight; for empty they came into the world, and empty too they seek to leave the world. But for the moment they are intoxicated. When they shake off their wine, then they will repent.

[71–F]   *Jesus said,* Where there are three gods, they are gods. Where there are two or one, I am with him.

[72–F]   *Jesus said,* No prophet is accepted in his own village; no physician heals those who know him.

[73–F]   *Jesus said,* Many times have you desired to hear these words which I am saying to you, and you have no one else to hear them from. There will be days when you will look for me and will not find me.

[74–F]   *His disciples said to him, 'Who are you, that you should say these things to us?' Jesus said to them, 'You do not realize who I am from* what I say to you, but you have become like the Jews, for they either love the tree and hate its fruit or love the fruit and hate the tree.

[75–F]   *His disciples said to him, 'Twenty-four prophets spoke in Israel, and all of them spoke in you.' He said to them,* You have omitted the one living in your presence and have spoken only of the dead.

[76–F]   *Jesus said,* It is to those who are worthy of My mysteries that I tell My mysteries. Do not let your left hand know what your right hand is doing.

[77–F]   *Jesus said,* I shall destroy this house, and no one will be able to rebuild it.

[78–F]   *Jesus said,* It is I who am the light which is above them all. It is I who am the All. From me did the All come forth, and unto me did the All extend. Split a piece of wood, and I am there. Lift up the stone, and you will find me there.

[79–F]   *Jesus said,* He who is near me is near the fire, and he who is far from me is far from the kingdom.

[80–F]   *Jesus said,* The foxes have their holes and the birds have their nests, but the Son of Man has no place to lay his head and rest.

[81–F]   *Jesus said,* Come unto me, for my yoke is easy and my lordship is mild, and you will find repose for yourselves.

[82–F]   *They said to Jesus, 'Come, let us pray today and let us fast.' Jesus said,* What is the sin that I have committed, or wherein have I been defeated? But when the bridegroom leaves the bridal chamber, then let them fast and pray.

[83–F] *Jesus said,* He who will drink from my mouth will become like me. I myself shall become he, and the things that are hidden will be revealed to him.

[84–G] And as long as I am with you, give heed to me and obey me; but when I depart from you, remember me. And remember me because I was with you and you did not know me. Blessed will they be who have known me; woe to those who have heard and have not believed. Blessed will they be who have not seen yet have believed.

[85–G] These are the things that I shall tell you so far; now, however, I shall ascend to the place from whence I came. But you, when I was eager to go, have cast me out, and instead of accompanying me, you have pursued me. But pay heed to the glory that awaits me and, having opened your heart, listen to the hymns that await me up in the heavens; for today I must take my place at the right hand of the Father.

[86–N] *The Savior said,* He Who Is is ineffable. No sovereignty knew him, no authority, no subjection, nor did any creature from the foundation of the world until now, except himself, and anyone to whom he wills to make revelation through him who is from the First Light. From now on I am the great Savior.

[87–N] But I came from the places above by the will of the great Light, I who escaped from that bond. I cut off the thing of the robbers. I wakened it, namely, that drop that was sent from Sophia, so that it might bear much fruit through me, and be perfected, and not be lacking, but be set apart by me, the great Savior, in order that his glory might be revealed, so that Sophia might also be justified in regard to that defect, so that her sons might not again become defective, but might attain honor and glory, and go up to their Father, and know the words of the masculine Light.

[88-N]   But I taught you about Immortal Man, and I loosed the bonds of the robbers from him. I broke the gates of the pitiless ones before their faces. I humiliated their malicious intent. They all were shamed and rose from their ignorance. Because of this, then, I came here, so that they might be joined with that spirit and breath, and might from two become one, just as from the first, so that you might yield much fruit and go up to the one who is from the beginning, in ineffable joy, and glory, and honor, and grace of the Father of the Universe.

[89-N]   I came from the First, who was sent so that I might reveal to you the one who is from the beginning, because of the arrogance of the Prime Begetter and his angels, because they say about themselves that they are gods. And I came to remove them from their blindness that I might tell everyone about the God who is above the universe. You, therefore, tread upon their graves, humiliate their malicious intent, and break their yoke, and arouse my own. I have given you authority over all things as sons of light, so that you might tread upon their power with your feet.

[90-O]   And the perfect Majesty is at rest in the ineffable light, in the truth of the mother of all these, and all of you that attain to me, to me alone who am perfect, because of the Word. For I exist with all the greatness of the Spirit, which is a friend to us and our kindred alike, since I brought forth a word to the glory of our Father, through his goodness, as well as an imperishable thought; that is, the Word within him — it is slavery that we shall die with Christ — and an imperishable and undefiled thought, an incomprehensible marvel, the writing of the ineffable water which is the word from us.

It is I who am in you, and you are in me, just as the Father is in you in innocence.

[91-O]   I visited a bodily dwelling. I cast out the one who was in it first, and I went in. And the whole multitude of the archons became troubled. And all the matter of the archons as well as all the begotten powers of the earth were shaken when it saw the likeness of the Image, since it was mixed. And I am the one who was in it, not resembling him who was in it first. For he was an earthly man, but I, I am from above the heavens. I did not refuse them even to become a Christ, but I did not reveal myself to them in the love which was coming forth from me. I revealed that I am a stranger to the regions below.

[92-O]   The whole greatness of the Fatherhood of the Spirit was at rest in his places. And I am he who was with him, since I have an Ennoia of a single emanation from the eternal ones and the undefiled and immeasurable incomprehensibilities. I placed the small Ennoia in the world, having disturbed them and frightened the whole multitude of the angels and their ruler. And I was visiting them all with fire and flame because of my Ennoia. And everything pertaining to them was brought about because of me. And there came about a disturbance and a fight around the Seraphim and Cherubim, since their glory will fade, and the confusion around Adonaios on both sides and their dwelling — to the Cosmocrator and him who said, 'Let us seize him'; others again, 'The plan will certainly not materialize.' For Adonaios knows me because of hope. And I was in the mouths of lions. And the plan which they devised about me to release their Error and their senselessness — I did not succumb to them as they had planned. But I was not afflicted at all. Those who were there punished me. And I did not die in reality but in appearance, lest I be put to shame by them because these are my kinsfolk. I removed the shame from me and I did not become faint-hearted in the face of what happened to me at their hands. I was about to succumb to fear, and I suffered according to their sight and thought, in order that they may never find any word to speak about them. For my death which they think happened, (happened) to them in their error and blindness, since they nailed their man unto their death. For their Ennoias did not see me, for they were deaf and blind. But in doing these things, they condemn themselves. Yes, they saw me; they punished me. It was another, their father, who drank the gall and the vinegar; it was not I. They struck me with the reed; it was another, Simon, who bore the cross on his shoulder. It was another upon whom they placed the crown of thorns. But I was rejoicing in the height over all the wealth of the archons and the offspring of their error, of their empty glory. And I was laughing at their ignorance.

[93-O]   And I subjected all their powers. For as I came downward no one saw me. For I was altering my shapes, changing from form to form. And therefore, when I was at their gates I assumed their likeness. For I passed them by quietly, and I was viewing the places, and I was not afraid nor ashamed, for I was undefiled. And I was speaking with them, mingling with them through those who are mine, and trampling on those who are harsh to them with zeal, and quenching the flame. And I was doing all these things because of my desire to accomplish what I desired by the will of the Father above.

[94-O]   I am Christ, the Son of Man, the one from you who is among you. I am despised for your sake, in order that you your-selves may forget the difference. And do not become female, lest you give birth to evil and its brothers: jealousy and division, anger and wrath, fear and a divided heart, and empty, non-existent desire. But I am an ineffable mystery to you.

[95-O]   It also happened in the places under heaven for their reconciliation. Those who knew me in salvation and undividedness, and those who existed for the glory of the father and the truth, having been separated, blended into the one through the living word. And I am in the spirit and the truth of the motherhood, just as he has been there; I was among those who are united in the friendship of friends forever, who neither know hostility at all, nor evil, but who are united by my Knowledge in word and peace which exists in perfection with everyone and in them all. And those who assumed the form of my type will assume the form of my word. Indeed, these will come forth in light forever, and (in) friendship with each other in the spirit, since they have known in every respect (and) indivisibly that what is is One. And all of these are one. And thus they will learn about the One, as (did) the Assembly and those dwelling in it. For the father of all these exists, being immeasurable (and) immutable: Nous and Word and Division and Envy and Fire. And he is entirely one, being the All with them all in a single doctrine because all these are from a single spirit. O unseeing ones, why did you not know the mystery rightly?

[96-Q]   *And as they were mourning and weeping, the Lord appeared to them and said to them,* For whom are you weeping? Now do not weep; I am he whom you seek. But let one of you go to your brothers and say to them, 'Come, our master has risen from the dead.'

[97-Q]   *And thus he said to us,* Come, and do not be afraid. I am your teacher whom you, Peter, denied three times before the cock crowed; and now do you deny again? *And we went to him thinking and doubting whether it was he. And he said to us,* Why do you doubt and why are you not believing? I am he who spoke to you concerning my flesh, my death, and my resurrection. And that you may know that it is I, lay your hand, Peter, and your finger in the nail-

print of my hands; and you, Thomas, in my side; and also you, An-
drew, see whether my foot steps on the ground and leaves a
footprint. For it is written in the prophet, 'But a ghost, a demon,
leaves no print on the ground.'

[98–Q]   While I was coming from the Father of all, passing by
the heavens, wherein I put on the wisdom of the Father and by his
power clothed myself in his power, I was in the heavens. And passing by the angels and archangels in their form and as one of them,
I passed by the orders, dominions, and princes, possessing the
measure of the wisdom of the Father who sent me. And the
archangels Michael and Gabriel, Raphael and Uriel followed me
until the fifth firmament of heaven, while I appeared as one of
them. This kind of power was given me by the Father. Then I
made the archangels to become distracted with the voice and go
up to the altar of the Father and serve the Father in his work until
I should return to him. I did this thus in the likeness of his wisdom. For I became all in all with them, that I, having . . . the will
of the mercy of the Father and perfected the glory of him who
sent me, might return to him.

[99–Q]   Do you not remember that I previously said to you that I
became like an angel to the angels? *And we said to him, 'Yes, O Lord.'
And he said to us,* At that time I appeared in the form of the
archangel Gabriel to the virgin Mary and spoke with her, and her
heart received me; she believed and laughed; and I, the Word, went
into her and became flesh; and I myself was servant for myself, and
in the form of the image of an angel; so I will do after I have gone to
my Father.

[100–Q]   Truly I say to you, I will come as the sun which bursts
forth; thus will I, shining seven times brighter than it in glory,

while I am carried on the wings of the clouds in splendor with my cross going on before me, come to the earth to judge the living and the dead.

[101–Q]   I am wholly in the Father and the Father in me. *Then we said to him, 'Will you really leave us until your coming? Where will we find a teacher?' And he answered and said to us,* Do you not know that until now I am both here and there with him who sent me? *And we said to him, 'O Lord, is it possible that you should be both here and there?' And he said to us,* I am wholly in the Father and the Father in me after his image and after his form and after his power and after his perfection and after his light, and I am his perfect word.

[102–Q]   And I am fully the right hand of the Father; I am in him who accomplishes.

[103–Q]   I have put on your flesh, in which I was born and died and was buried and rose again through my heavenly Father, that it might be fulfilled that was said by the prophet David concerning my death and resurrection: 'O Lord, how numerous have they become that oppress me; many have risen up against me. Many say to my soul, "He has no salvation by his God." But you, O Lord, are my refuge, my glory, and he who lifts up my head.'

[104–Q]   And for this cause have I perfected all mercy; without being begotten I was born of man, and without having flesh I put on flesh and grew up, that I might regenerate you who were begotten in the flesh, and in regeneration you obtain the resurrection in your flesh, a garment that will not pass away, with all who hope and believe in him who sent me; for my Father has found pleasure in you; and to whoever I will I give the hope of the kingdom.

[105-Q]   Truly I say to you that I have received all power from my Father that I may bring back those in darkness into light and those in corruptibility into incorruptibility and those in error into righteousness and those in death into life, and that those in captivity may be loosed, as what is impossible on the part of men is possible on the part of the Father. I am the hope of the hopeless, the helper of those who have no helper, the treasure of those in need, the physician of the sick, the resurrection of the dead.

[106-R]   For what you are, that I have shown you, as you see; but what I am is known to me alone, and no one else. Let me have what is mine; what is yours you must see through me; but me you must see truly — not that which I am, as I said, but that which you, as my kinsman, are able to know. You hear that I suffered, yet I suffered not; and that I suffered not, yet I did suffer; and that I was pierced, yet I was not wounded; that I was hanged, yet I was not hanged; that blood flowed from me, yet it did not flow, and, in a word, that what they say of me, I did not endure, but what they do not say, those things I did suffer. Now what these are, I secretly show you; for I know that you will understand. You must know me, then, as the torment of the Logos, the piercing of the Logos, the blood of the Logos, the wounding of the Logos, the fastening of the Logos, the death of the Logos. And so I speak, discarding the manhood. The first then that you must know is the Logos; then you shall know the Lord; and thirdly the man, and what he has suffered.

[107-S]   *And they asked and besought him: Lord, show us the secrets of the heaven. But Jesus answered*: I can reveal nothing to you before I have put off this body of flesh.

[108-S]   *When Bartholomew had uttered this prayer, Jesus said to him*: Bartholomew, the Father named me Christ, that I might come

IV

Warnings and Admonitions

[1–A] Whoever therefore breaks one of the least of these commandments, and teaches men so, shall be called least in the kingdom of heaven; but whoever does and teaches them, he shall be called great in the kindom of heaven.

[2–A] You have heard that it was said to those of old, 'You shall not murder, and whoever murders will be in danger of the judgment.' But I say to you that whoever is angry with his brother without a cause shall be in danger of the judgment. And whoever says to his brother, 'Raca!' shall be in danger of the council. But whoever says, 'You fool!' shall be in danger of hell fire.

[3–A] You have heard that it was said to those of old, 'You shall not commit adultery.' But I say to you that whoever looks at a woman to lust for her has already committed adultery with her in his heart.

[4-A]   For if you forgive men their trespasses, your heavenly Father will also forgive you. But if you do not forgive men their trespasses, neither will your Father forgive your trespasses.

[5-A]   Do not lay up for yourselves treasures on earth, where moth and rust destroy and where thieves break in and steal; but lay up for yourselves treasures in heaven, where neither moth nor rust destroys and where thieves do not break in and steal. For where your treasure is, there your heart will be also.

[6-A]   Enter by the narrow gate; for wide is the gate and broad is the way that leads to destruction, and there are many who go in by it. Because narrow is the gate and difficult is the way which leads to life, and there are few who find it.

[7-A]   Not everyone who says to Me, 'Lord, Lord,' shall enter the kingdom of heaven, but he who does the will of My Father in heaven. Many will say to Me in that day, 'Lord, Lord, have we not prophesied in Your name, cast out demons in Your name, and done many wonders in Your name?' And then I will declare to them, 'I never knew you; depart from Me, you who practice lawlessness!'

[8-A]   And whoever will not receive you nor hear your words, when you depart from that house or city, shake off the dust from your feet. Assuredly, I say to you, it will be more tolerable for the land of Sodom and Gomorrah in the day of judgment than for that city!

[9-A]   Behold, I send you out as sheep in the midst of wolves. Therefore be wise as serpents and harmless as doves. But beware of men, for they will deliver you up to councils and scourge you in their synagogues. You will be brought before governors and kings for My sake, as a testimony to them and to the Gentiles.

[10–A]   Are not two sparrows sold for a copper coin? And not one of them falls to the ground apart from your Father's will. But the very hairs of your head are all numbered. Do not fear therefore; you are of more value than many sparrows. Therefore whoever confesses Me before men, him I will also confess before My Father who is in heaven. But whoever denies Me before men, him I will also deny before My Father who is in heaven.

[11–A]   Do not think that I came to bring peace on earth. I did not come to bring peace but a sword. For I have come to 'set a man against his father, a daughter against her mother, and a daughter-in-law against her mother-in-law'; and 'a man's enemies will be those of his own household.' He who loves father or mother more than Me is not worthy of Me. And he who loves son or daughter more than Me is not worthy of Me. And he who does not take his cross and follow after Me is not worthy of Me. He who finds his life will lose it, and he who loses his life for My sake will find it.

[12–A]   Woe to you, Chorazin! Woe to you, Bethsaida! For if the mighty works which were done in you had been done in Tyre and Sidon, they would have repented long ago in sackcloth and ashes. But I say to you, it will be more tolerable for Tyre and Sidon in the day of judgment than for you. And you, Capernaum, who are exalted to heaven, will be brought down to Hades; for if the mighty works which were done in you had been done in Sodom, it would have remained until this day. But I say to you that it shall be more tolerable for the land of Sodom in the day of judgment than for you.

[13–A]   He who is not with Me is against me, and he who does not gather with Me scatters abroad.

[14-A]   Therefore I say to you, every sin and blasphemy will be forgiven men, but the blasphemy against the Spirit will not be forgiven men. Anyone who speaks a word against the Son of Man, it will be forgiven him; but whoever speaks against the Holy Spirit, it will not be forgiven him, either in this age or in the age to come. Either make the tree good and its fruit good, or else make the tree bad and its fruit bad; for a tree is known by its fruit.

[15-A]   Brood of vipers! How can you, being evil, speak good things? For out of the abundance of the heart the mouth speaks. A good man out of the good treasure of his heart brings forth good things, and an evil man out of the evil treasure brings forth evil things.

[16-A]   When an unclean spirit goes out of a man, he goes through dry places, seeking rest, and finds none. Then he says, 'I will return to my house from which I came.' And when he comes, he finds it empty, swept, and put in order. Then he goes and takes with him seven spirits more wicked than himself, and they enter and dwell there; and the last state of that man is worse than the first. So shall it also be with this wicked generation.

[17-A]   Not what goes into the mouth defiles a man; but what comes out of the mouth, this defiles a man.

[18-A]   For out of the heart proceed evil thoughts, murders, adulteries, fornications, thefts, false witness, blasphemies. These are the things which defile a man, but to eat with unwashed hands does not defile a man.

[19-A]   A wicked and adulterous generation seeks after a sign, and no sign shall be given to it except the sign of the prophet Jonah.

[20–A]   *Then Jesus said to them,* Take heed and beware of the leaven of the Pharisees and of the Sadducees.

[21–A]   Woe to the world because of offenses! For offenses must come, but woe to that man by whom the offense comes!

[22–A]   Take heed that you do not despise one of these little ones, for I say to you that in heaven their angels always see the face of My Father who is in heaven. For the Son of man has come to save that which was lost.

[23–A]   And I say to you, whoever divorces his wife, except for sexual immorality, and marries another, commits adultery; and whoever marries her who is divorced commits adultery.

[24–A]   And whoever exalts himself will be humbled, and he who humbles himself will be exalted.

[25–A]   But woe to you, scribes and Pharisees, hypocrites! For you shut up the kingdom of heaven against men; for you neither go in yourselves, nor do you allow those who are entering to go in.

[26–A]   Woe to you, scribes and Pharisees, hypocrites! For you devour widows' houses, and for a pretense make long prayers. Therefore you will receive greater condemnation.

[27–A]   Woe to you, scribes and Pharisees, hypocrites! For you travel land and sea to win one proselyte, and when he is won, you make him twice as much a son of hell as yourselves.

[28–A]   Woe to you, blind guides, who say, 'Whoever swears by the temple, it is nothing; but whoever swears by the gold of the temple, he is obliged to perform it.' Fools and blind! For which is greater, the gold or the temple that sanctifies the gold?

[29-A]   And, 'Whoever swears by the altar, it is nothing; but whoever swears by the gift that is on it, he is obliged to perform it.' Fools and blind! For which is greater, the gift or the altar that sanctifies the gift? Therefore he who swears by the altar, swears by it and by all things on it. He who swears by the temple, swears by it and by Him who dwells in it. And he who swears by heaven, swears by the throne of God and by Him who sits on it.

[30-A]   Woe to you, scribes and Pharisees, hypocrites! For you pay tithe of mint and anise and cummin, and have neglected the weightier matters of the law: justice and mercy and faith. These you ought to have done, without leaving the others undone. Blind guides, who strain out a gnat and swallow a camel!

[31-A]   Woe to you, scribes and Pharisees, hypocrites! For you cleanse the outside of the cup and dish, but inside they are full of extortion and self-indulgence. Blind Pharisee, first cleanse the inside of the cup and dish, that the outside of them may be clean also.

[32-A]   Woe to you, scribes and Pharisees, hypocrites! For you are like whitewashed tombs which indeed appear beautiful outwardly, but inside are full of dead men's bones and all uncleanness. Even so you also outwardly appear righteous to men, but inside you are full of hypocrisy and lawlessness.

[33-A]   Woe to you, scribes and Pharisees, hypocrites! Because you build the tombs of the prophets and adorn the monuments of the righteous, and say, 'If we had lived in the days of our fathers, we would not have been partakers with them in the blood of the prophets.' Therefore you are witnesses against yourselves that you are sons of those who murdered the prophets. Fill up, then, the measure of your fathers' guilt. Serpents, brood of vipers! How can you escape the condemnation of hell?

[34–A]   *But Jesus said to him*, Put your sword in its place, for all who take the sword will perish by the sword.

[35–B]   Take heed what you hear; the measure you give will be the measure you get, and still more will be given you.

[36–B]   Well did Isaiah prophesy of you hypocrites, as it is written, 'This people honors me with their lips, but their heart is far from me; in vain do they worship me, teaching as doctrines the precepts of men.' You leave the commandment of God, and hold fast the tradition of men.

[37–B]   You have a fine way of rejecting the commandment of God, in order to keep your tradition! For Moses said, 'Honor your father and your mother'; and, 'He who speaks evil of father or mother, let him surely die'; but you say, 'If a man tells his father or his mother, What you would have gained from me is Corban' (that is, given to God) — then you no longer permit him to do anything for his father or mother, thus making void the word of God through your tradition which you hand on. And many such things you do.

[38–B]   *And he called the people to him again, and said to them*, Hear me, all of you, and understand: there is nothing outside a man which by going into him can defile him; but the things which come out of a man are what defile him.

[39–B]   Get behind me, Satan! For you are not on the side of God, but of men.

[40–B]   *John said to him, 'Teacher, we saw a man casting out demons in your name, and we forbade him, because he was not following us.' But Jesus said,* Do not forbid him; for no one who does a mighty work in my name will be able soon after to speak evil of me. For he that is not against us is for us. For truly, I say to you, whoever gives you a cup of water to drink because you bear the name of Christ, will by no means lose his reward.

[41–B]   Whoever causes one of these little ones who believe in me to sin, it would be better for him if a great millstone were hung round his neck and he were thrown into the sea. And if your hand causes you to sin, cut it off; it is better for you to enter life maimed than with two hands to go to hell, to the unquenchable fire. And if your foot causes you to sin, cut it off; it is better for you to enter life lame than with two feet to be thrown into hell.

[42–B]   And if your eye causes you to sin, pluck it out; it is better for you to enter the kingdom of God with one eye than with two eyes to be thrown into hell, where their worm does not die, and the fire is not quenched. For every one will be salted with fire. Salt is good; but if the salt has lost its saltness, how will you season it? Have salt in yourselves, and be at peace with one another.

[43–B]   *And Jesus looked around and said to his disciples,* How hard it will be for those who have riches to enter the kingdom of God!

[44–C]   Those who are well have no need of a physician, but those who are sick; I have not come to call the righteous, but sinners to repentance.

[45-C]   But woe to you who are rich, for you have received your consolation.

[46-C]   Woe to you who are full, for you shall hunger. Woe to you who laugh now, for you shall mourn and weep.

[47-C]   Woe to you when all men speak well of you, for so did their fathers to the false prophets.

[48-C]   This is an evil generation. It seeks a sign, and no sign will be given to it except the sign of Jonah the prophet. For as Jonah became a sign to the Ninevites, so also the Son of Man will be to this generation.

[49-C]   *And He said,* Woe to you also, lawyers! For you load men with burdens hard to bear, and you yourselves do not touch the burdens with one of your fingers.

[50-C]   Therefore the wisdom of God also said, 'I will send them prophets and apostles, and some of them they will kill and persecute,' that the blood of all the prophets which was shed from the foundation of the world may be required of this generation, from the blood of Abel to the blood of Zechariah who perished between the altar and the temple. Yes, I say to you, it shall be required of this generation.

[51-C]   Woe to you lawyers! For you have taken away the key of knowledge. You did not enter in yourselves, and those who were entering in you hindered.

[52-C]   Beware of the leaven of the Pharisees, which is hypocrisy. For there is nothing covered that will not be revealed, nor hidden that will not be known. Therefore whatever you have spoken in the dark will be heard in the light, and what you have spoken in the ear in inner rooms will be proclaimed on the housetops.

[53–C]   And I say to you, My friends, do not be afraid of those who kill the body, and after that have no more that they can do. But I will show you whom you should fear: Fear Him who, after He has killed, has power to cast into hell; yes, I say to you, Fear Him! Are not five sparrows sold for two copper coins? And not one of them is forgotten before God. But the very hairs of your head are all numbered. Do not fear therefore; you are of more value than many sparrows.

[54–C]   Also I say to you, whoever confesses Me before men, him the Son of Man also will confess before the angels of God. But he who denies Me before men will be denied before the angels of God.

[55–C]   *And He said to them,* Take heed and beware of covetousness, for one's life does not consist in the abundance of the things he possesses.

[56–C]   Let your waist be girded and your lamps burning; and you yourselves be like men who wait for their master, when he will return from the wedding, that when he comes and knocks they may open to him immediately. Blessed are those servants whom the master, when he comes, will find watching. Assuredly, I say to you that he will gird himself and have them sit down to eat, and will come and serve them. And if he should come in the second watch, or come in the third watch, and find them so, blessed are those servants.

[57–C]   But know this, that if the master of the house had known what hour the thief would come, he would have watched and not allowed his house to be broken into. Therefore you also be ready, for the Son of Man is coming at an hour you do not expect.

[58–C]   I came to send fire on the earth, and how I wish it were already kindled!

[59–C]   When you go with your adversary to the magistrate, make every effort along the way to settle with him, lest he drag you to the judge, the judge deliver you to the officer, and the officer throw you into prison. I tell you, you shall not depart from there till you have paid the very last mite.

[60–C]   *Then He said to the disciples,* It is impossible that no offenses should come, but woe to him through whom they do come! It would be better for him if a millstone were hung around his neck, and he were thrown into the sea, than that he should offend one of these little ones.

[61–D]   *Jesus said to them,* The light is with you for a little longer. Walk while you have the light, lest the darkness overtake you; he who walks in the darkness does not know where he goes.

[62–F]   *Jesus said,* If those who lead you say to you, 'See, the Kingdom is in the sky,' then the birds of the sky will precede you. If they say to you, 'It is in the sea,' then the fish will precede you. Rather, the Kingdom is inside of you, and it is outside of you. When you come to know yourselves, then you will become known, and you will realize that it is you who are the sons of the living Father. But if you will not know yourselves, you dwell in poverty and it is you who are that poverty.

[63–F] *Jesus said to them,* If you fast, you will give rise to sin for yourselves; and if you pray, you will be condemned; and if you give alms, you will do harm to your spirits. When you go into any land and walk about in the districts, if they receive you, eat what they will set before you, and heal the sick among them. For what goes into your mouth will not defile you, but that which issues from your mouth — it is that which will defile you.

[64–F] *Jesus said,* I shall give you what no eye has seen and what no ear has heard and what no hand has touched and what has never occurred to the human mind.

[65–F] *Jesus said,* If you do not fast as regards the world, you will not find the Kingdom. If you do not observe the Sabbath as a Sabbath, you will not see the Father.

[66–F] *They saw a Samaritan carrying a lamb on his way to Judea. He said to his disciples,* Why does that man carry the lamb around? *They said to Him, 'So that he may kill it and eat it.' He said to them,* You too, look for a place for yourselves within Repose, lest you become a corpse and be eaten.

[67–F] *Jesus said,* That which you have will save you if you bring it forth from yourselves. That which you do not have within you will kill you if you do not have it within you.

[68–F] *Jesus said,* Wretched is the body that is dependent upon a body, and wretched is the soul that is dependent on these two.

[69–F] *Jesus said,* Why do you wash the outside of the cup? Do you not realize that he who made the inside is the same one who made the outside?

[70-F]   *Jesus said*, Do not give what is holy to dogs, lest they throw them on the dung-heap. Do not throw the pearls to swine, lest they grind it to bits.

[71-F]   *Jesus said*, Woe to the flesh that depends on the soul; woe to the soul that depends on the flesh.

[72-G]   Woe to those who have seen the son of man; blessed will they be who have not seen the man, and they who have not consorted with him, and they who have not spoken with him, and they who have not listened to anything from him: yours is life! Know, then, that he healed you when you were ill that you might reign. Woe to those who have found relief from their illness, for they will relapse into illness. Blessed will they be who have not been ill, and have known relief before falling ill: yours is the kingdom of God. Therefore I say to you, become full and leave no space within you empty, for he who is coming can mock you.

[73-G]   What is your merit if you do the will of the Father and it is not given to you from him as a gift while you are tempted by Satan? But if you are oppressed by Satan and persecuted and you do his (the Father's) will, I say that he will love you, and make you equal with me, and reckon you to have become beloved through his providence by your own choice. So will you not cease loving the flesh and being afraid of sufferings? Or do you not know that you have yet to be abused and to be accused unjustly; and have yet to be shut up in prison, and condemned unlawfully, and crucified without reason, and buried shamefully, as was I myself, by the evil one? Do you dare to spare the flesh, you for whom the Spirit is an encircling wall? If you consider how long the world existed before you, and how long it will exist after you, you will find that your life is one single day and your sufferings one single hour. For the good will not enter into the world. Scorn death, therefore, and take thought for life! Remember my cross and my death, and you will live!

[74-G]   Verily I say unto you, none will be saved unless they believe in my cross. But those who have believed in my cross, theirs is the kingdom of God. Therefore become seekers for death, like the dead who seek for life, for that which they seek is revealed to them. And what is there to trouble them? As for you, when you examine death, it will teach you election. Verily I say unto you, none of those who fear death will be saved; for the kingdom of death belongs to those who put themselves to death. Become better than I; make yourselves like the son of the Holy Spirit!

[75-G]   O you wretches; O you unfortunates; O you pretenders to the truth; O you falsifiers of knowledge; O you sinners against the Spirit: can you still bear to listen when it behooved you to speak from the first? Can you still bear to sleep, when it behooved you to be awake from the first, so that the kingdom of heaven might receive you? Verily I say unto you, it is easier for a pure one to fall into defilement, and for a man of light to fall into darkness, than for you to reign or not reign.

[76-G]   Woe to you, you who lack an advocate! Woe to you, you who stand in need of grace! Blessed will they be who have spoken out and obtained grace for themselves. Liken yourselves to foreigners; of what sort are they in the eyes of your city? Why are you disturbed when you cast yourselves away of your own accord and separate yourselves from your city? Why do you abandon your dwelling place of your own accord, making it ready for those who want to dwell in it? O you outcasts and fugitives: woe to you, for you will be caught! Or do you perhaps think that the Father is a lover of mankind, or that he is won over without prayers, or that he grants remission to one on another's behalf, or that he bears with one who asks? — For he knows the desire and also what it is that the flesh needs! — Or do you think that it is not this flesh that desires the soul? For without the soul the body does not sin, just as the soul is not saved without the spirit. But if the soul is saved when it is without evil, and the spirit is also saved, then the body becomes free from sin. For it is the spirit that quickens the soul, but the body that kills it; that is, it is it (the soul) which kills itself. Verily I say unto you, he will not forgive the soul the sin by any means, nor the flesh the guilt; for none of those who have worn the flesh will be saved. For do you think that many have found the kingdom of heaven? Blessed is he who has seen himself as a fourth one in heaven!

[77-G]   Verily I say unto you, woe to those for whose sakes I was sent down to this place; blessed will they be who ascend to the Father. Once more I reprove you, you who are: become like those who are not, that you may be with those who are not.

[78-H]   He who shall not eat my flesh and drink my blood has not life in him.

[79-H]   Every plant which my father who is in heaven has not planted will be plucked out.

[80-I]   O unsearchable love of the light! O bitterness of the fire that burns in the bodies of men and in their marrow, burning in them night and day, burning in the limbs of men and making their minds drunk and their souls deranged and moving them within males and females by day and night and moving them with a movement that moves secretly and visibly. For the males move; they move upon the females and the females upon the males. Therefore it is said, 'Everyone who seeks the truth from true wisdom will make himself wings so as to fly, fleeing the lust that scorches the spirits of men.' And he will make himself wings to flee every visible spirit.

[81-I]   Therefore it is necessary for us to speak to you, since this is the doctrine for the perfect. If, now, you desire to become perfect, you shall observe these things; if not, your name is 'Ignorant,' since it is impossible for a wise man to dwell with a fool, for the wise man is perfect in all wisdom. To the fool, however, the good and bad are the same — for 'the wise man will be nourished by the truth' and 'will be like a tree growing by the meandering stream' — seeing that there are some who, although having wings, rush upon the visible things, things that are far from the truth. For that which guides them, the fire, will give them an illusion of truth, and will shine on them with a perishable beauty, and it will imprison them in a dark sweetness and captivate them with fragrant pleasure. And it will blind them with insatiable lust and burn their souls and become for them like a stake stuck in their heart which they can never dislodge. And like a bit in the mouth it leads them according to its own desire. It has fettered them with its chains and bound all their limbs with the bitter bond of lust for those visible things that will decay and change and swerve by impulse. They have always been attracted downwards: as they are killed, they are assimilated to all the beasts of the perishable realm.

[82-I]   *Thomas answered and said, 'Is it good for us, Lord, to rest among our own?' The Savior said,* Yes, it is useful. And it is good for you since things visible among men will dissolve — for the vessel of their flesh will dissolve, and when it is brought to naught it will come to be among visible things, among things that are seen. And then the fire which they see gives them pain on account of love for the faith they formerly possessed. They will be gathered back to that which is visible. Moreover, those who see among things that are not visible, without the first love they will perish in the concern for this life and the scorching in the fire. Only a little time until that which is visible dissolves; then shapeless shades will emerge and in the midst of tombs they will forever dwell upon the corpses in pain and corruption of soul.

[83-I]   Truly I tell you that he who will listen to your word and turn away his face or sneer at it or smirk at these things, truly I tell you that he will be handed over to the Ruler above who rules over all the powers as their king, and he will turn that one around and cast him from heaven down to the abyss, and he will be imprisoned in a narrow dark place. Moreover, he can neither turn nor move on account of the great depth of Tartaros and the heavy bitterness of Hades that besets him. They are imprisoned in it in order that they might not escape — their madness will not be forgiven. And the Rulers who will pursue you will deliver them over to the angel Tartarouchos and he will take whips of fire, pursuing them with fiery scourges that cast a shower of sparks into the face of the one who is pursued. If he flees westward, he finds the fire. If he flees southward, he finds it there as well. If he turns northward, the threat of seething fire meets him again. Nor does he find the way to the East so as to flee there and be saved, for he did not find it in the day he was in the body, so that he will find it in the day of Judgment.

[84-I]   Woe to you, godless ones, who have no hope, who rely on things that will not happen! Woe to you who hope in the flesh and in the prison that will perish! How long will you be oblivious? And the imperishables, do you think that they will perish too? Your hope is set upon the world and your god is this life! You are corrupting your souls!

[85-I]   Woe to you for the fire that burns in you, for it is insatiable!

[86–I]   Woe to you because of the wheel that turns in your minds!

[87–I]   Woe to you because of the burning that is in you, for it will devour your flesh openly and rend your souls secretly, and prepare you for your companions!

[88–I]   Woe to you, captives, for you are bound in caverns! You laugh! In mad laughter you rejoice! You neither realize your perdition, nor do you reflect on your circumstances, nor have you understood that you dwell in darkness and death! On the contrary, you are drunk with the fire and full of bitterness. Your mind is deranged on account of the burning that is in you, and sweet to you is the crown of your enemies' blows! And the darkness rose for you like the light, for you surrendered your freedom for servitude! You darkened your hearts and surrendered your thoughts to folly, and you filled your thoughts with the smoke of the fire that is in you! And your light has hidden in the cloud of darkness and the garment that is put upon you, you pursued deceitfully and you were seized by the hope that does not exist. And whom is it you have believed? Do you not know that you all dwell among those who want you to curse yourselves as if your hope were nonexistent? You baptized your souls in the water of darkness! You walked by your own whims!

[89–I]   Woe to you who love intimacy with womankind and polluted intercourse with it!

[90–I]   And woe to you because of the powers of your body, for those will afflict you!

[91–I]   Woe to you because of the forces of the evil demons!

[92-I] Woe to you who beguile your limbs with the fire! Who is it that will rain a refreshing dew on you to extinguish the mass of fire from you along with your burning? Who is it that will cause the sun to shine upon you to disperse the darkness in you and hide the darkness and polluted water?

[93-I] *Then Jesus continued and said,* Woe to you, for you did not receive the doctrine, and those who are ignorant will labor at preaching instead of you, and you are rushing into profligacy. Yet there are some who have been sent down to rescue all those whom you killed daily in order that they might rise from death.

[94-J] I have told you, 'Leave the blind alone!' And you, see how they do not know what they are saying. For the son of their glory instead of my servant they have put to shame.

[95-K] *When the blessed one had said this, he greeted them all, saying,* Peace be with you. Receive my peace to yourselves. Beware that no one lead you astray, saying, 'Lo here!' or 'Lo there!' For the Son of Man is within you. Follow after him! Those who seek him will find him. Go then and preach the gospel of the kingdom. Do not lay down any rules beyond what I appointed for you, and do not give a law like the lawgiver lest you be constrained by it.

[96-M] *The Lord said,* Everything which I have said to you you have understood and received in faith. If you have known them, they are yours; if not, they are not yours.

[97-N] Everything that came from the perishable will perish, since they came from the perishable. And whatever came from imperishableness does not perish but becomes imperishable. Thus a multitude of men went astray; since they did not know this difference, they died.

[98-O]   After we went forth from our home, and came down to this world, and came into being in the world in bodies, we were hated and persecuted, not only by those who are ignorant, but also by those who think that they are advancing the name of Christ, since they were unknowingly empty, not knowing who they are, like dumb animals. They persecuted those who have been liberated by me, since they hate them — those who, should they shut their mouth, would weep with a profitless groaning because they did not fully know me. Instead, they served two masters, even a multitude. But you will become victorious in everything, in war and battles, jealous division and wrath. But in the uprightness of our love we are innocent, pure, (and) good, since we have a mind of the Father in an ineffable mystery.

[99-O]   O those who do not see, you do not see your blindness, i.e. this which was not known, nor has it ever been known, nor has it been known about him. They did not listen to firm obedience. Therefore they proceeded in a judgment of error, and they raised their defiled and murderous hands against him as if they were beating the air. And the senseless and blind ones are always senseless, always being slaves of law and earthly fear.

[100-Q]   *And he said to us, being angry,* You of little faith, how long yet do you ask me? And inquire only without anguish after what you wish to hear. Keep my commandments, and do what I tell you, without delay and without reserve and without respect of persons; serve in the straight, direct, and narrow way. And thereby will the Father in every respect rejoice concerning you.

[101-Q]   And on that account I have descended and have spoken with Abraham and Isaac and Jacob, to your fathers the prophets, and have brought to them news that they may come from the rest which is below into heaven, and have given them the right hand of the baptism of life and forgiveness and pardon for all wickedness as to you, so from now on also to those who believe in me. But whoever believes in me and does not do my commandment receives, although he believes in my name, no benefit from it. He has run a course in vain. His end is determined for ruin and for punishment of great pain, for he has sinned against my commandment.

[102-Q]   But those who have sinned against my commandment, who teach something else, subtract from and add to and work for their own glory, alienating those who rightly believe in me, I will deliver them to ruin.

[103-Q]   And whoever has believed in me will live, if he has done the work of light. But if he acknowledges that it is light and does what is characteristic of darkness, then he has neither anything that he can say in defense nor will he be able to raise his face and look at the son, which Son I am. And I will say to him, 'You have sought and found, have asked and received. What do you blame us for? Why did you withdraw from me and my kingdom? You have acknowledged me and yet denied.' Now therefore see that each one is able to live as well as to die.

[104-Q]   But if someone should fall bearing his burden, i.e. the sin he has committed against the person of his neighbor, then his neighbor should admonish him in return for what good he has done to his neighbor. And when his neighbor has admonished him and he has returned, then he will be saved, and he who has admonished him will obtain eternal life. But if he sees how this one who renders him service sins, and encourages him, such a one will be judged in a great judgment. For a blind man who leads a blind man, both will fall into a ditch. Even so the one who encourages, who respects the person, and also the one whom he encourages and whose person he respects, will both be punished with one punishment, as the prophet said, 'Woe to those who encourage, who speak fair to the sinner for the sake of a bribe, whose God is their belly.' You see how the judgment is? Truly I say to you, in that day I will not fear the rich and will have no pity for the poor.

[105–Q]   . . . Who thus hate, and he who loves me and finds fault with those who do not do my commandments, these will thus be hated and persecuted, and men will despise and mock them. They will also deliberately say what is not true, and there will come a conspiracy against those who love me. But these will rebuke them that they may be saved. And those who will find fault with them and correct and exhort them will be hated and set apart and despised; and those who wish to do good to them will be prevented from it. But those who have endured this will be as martyrs with the Father, for they were zealous concerning righteousness and were not zealous with corruptible zeal.

[106–S]   *And they asked and besought him; 'Lord, show us the secrets of the Heaven.' But Jesus answered*: I can reveal nothing to you before I have put off this body of flesh.

[107–U]   *And our Lord answered and said to us*, Take heed that men deceive you not and that ye do not become doubters and serve other gods. Many will come in my name saying, 'I am Christ.' Believe them not and draw not near unto them.

[108–U]   O Peter, why speakest thou thus, 'that not to have been created were better for them?' Thou resistest God. Thou wouldest not have more compassion than he for his image, for he has created them and has brought them forth when they were not. And since thou hast seen the lamentation which sinners shall encounter in the last days, therefore thy heart is saddened; but I will show thee their works in which they have sinned against the Most High.

[109–U]   Satan maketh war against thee, and has veiled thine understanding, and the good things of this world conquer thee. Thine eyes must be opened and thine ears unstopped that . . . a tabernacle, which the hand of man has not made, but which my heavenly Father has made for me and for the elect.

[110–V]   Though you should be joined to me in my bosom and keep not my commandments, I will cast you out and say to you: Depart from me, I know you not, whence you are, you doers of lawlessness.

[111–V]   If you have not kept what is little, who will give you what is great? For I say to you: He who is faithful in what is least, is faithful also in much.

[112–X]   Woe, woe unto the souls that despise their own judgment! For I see men who delight their souls in vanity and abandon themselves to the unclean world. I see also how all that is for the benefit of the enemy! Therefore I can stand by them and say: O souls that apply yourselves to unchastity and have no fear before God!

[113–X]   Depart from me, ye evil-doers, I know you not: so will I speak to those who go into destruction.

V

Teachings and Proverbs

[1–A] Blessed are the poor in spirit, for theirs is the kingdom of heaven.

Blessed are those who mourn, for they shall be comforted.

Blessed are the meek, for they shall inherit the earth.

Blessed are those who hunger and thirst for righteousness, for they shall be filled.

Blessed are the merciful, for they shall obtain mercy.

Blessed are the pure in heart, for they shall see God.

Blessed are the peacemakers, for they shall be called sons of God.

Blessed are those who are persecuted for righteousness' sake, for theirs is the kingdom of heaven.

Blessed are you when they revile and persecute you, and say all kinds of evil against you falsely for My sake.

Rejoice and be exceedingly glad, for great is your reward in heaven, for so they persecuted the prophets who were before you.

[2–A]   You are the light of the world. A city that is set on a hill cannot be hidden. Nor do they light a lamp and put it under a basket, but on a lampstand, and it gives light to all who are in the house. Let your light so shine before men, that they may see your good works and glorify your Father in heaven.

[3–A]   For assuredly, I say to you, till heaven and earth pass away, one jot or one tittle will by no means pass from the law till all is fulfilled.

[4–A]   For I say to you, that unless your righteousness exceeds the righteousness of the scribes and Pharisees, you will by no means enter the kingdom of heaven.

[5–A]   Therefore if you bring your gift to the altar, and there remember that your brother has something against you, leave your gift there before the altar, and go your way. First be reconciled to your brother, and then come and offer your gift. Agree with your adversary quickly, while you are on the way with him, lest your adversary deliver you to the judge, the judge hand you over to the officer, and you be thrown into prison. Assuredly, I say to you, you will by no means get out of there till you have paid the last penny.

[6–A]   You have heard that it was said, 'An eye for an eye and a tooth for a tooth.' But I tell you not to resist an evil person. But whoever slaps you on your right cheek, turn the other to him also. If anyone wants to sue you and take away your tunic, let him have your cloak also. And whoever compels you to go one mile, go with him two.

[7–A]   For if you love those who love you, what reward have you? Do not even the tax collectors do the same? And if you greet your brethren only, what do you do more than others? Do not even the tax collectors do so? Therefore you shall be perfect, just as your Father in heaven is perfect.

[8-A]   And when you pray, you shall not be like the hypocrites. For they love to pray standing in the synagogues and on the corners of the streets, that they may be seen by men. Assuredly, I say to you, they have their reward. But you, when you pray, go into your room, and when you have shut your door, pray to your Father who is in the secret place; and your Father who sees in secret will reward you openly.

[9-A]   And when you pray, do not use vain repetitions as the heathen do. For they think that they will be heard for their many words. Therefore do not be like them. For your Father knows the things you have need of before you ask Him.

[10-A]   The lamp of the body is the eye. If therefore your eye is good, your whole body will be full of light. But if your eye is bad, your whole body will be full of darkness. If therefore the light that is in you is darkness, how great is that darkness!

[11-A]   Therefore I say to you, do not worry about your life, what you will eat or what you will drink; nor about your body, what you will put on. Is not life more than food and the body more than clothing? Look at the birds of the air, for they neither sow nor reap nor gather into barns; yet your heavenly Father feeds them. Are you not of more value than they?

[12-A]   Which of you by worrying can add one cubit to his stature? So why do you worry about clothing? Consider the lilies of the field, how they grow: they neither toil or spin; and yet I say to you that even Solomon in all his glory was not arrayed like one of these. Now if God so clothes the grass of the field, which today is, and tomorrow is thrown into the oven, will He not much more clothe you, O you of little faith?

[13–A]   Therefore do not worry, saying, 'What shall we eat?' or 'What shall we drink?' or 'What shall we wear?' For after all these things the Gentiles seek. For your heavenly Father knows that you need all these things.

[14–A]   But seek first the kingdom of God and His righteousness, and all these things shall be added to you. Therefore do not worry about tomorrow, for tomorrow will worry about its own things. Sufficient for the day is its own trouble.

[15–A]   Judge not, that you be not judged.

[16–A]   Ask, and it will be given to you; seek, and you will find; knock, and it will be opened to you. For everyone who asks receives, and he who seeks finds, and to him who knocks it will be opened.

[17–A]   Or what man is there among you who, if his son asks for bread, will give him a stone? Or if he asks for a fish, will he give him a serpent? If you then, being evil, know how to give good gifts to your children, how much more will your Father who is in heaven give good things to those who ask Him! Therefore, whatever you want men to do to you, do also to them, for this is the Law and the Prophets.

[18–A]   Beware of false prophets, who come to you in sheep's clothing, but inwardly they are ravenous wolves. You will know them by their fruits. Do men gather grapes from thornbushes or figs from thistles?

[19-A]   Follow Me, and let the dead bury their own dead.

[20-A]   Those who are well have no need of a physician, but those who are sick. But go and learn what this means: 'I desire mercy and not sacrifice.' For I did not come to call the righteous, but sinners, to repentance.

[21-A]   The harvest truly is plentiful, but the laborers are few. Therefore pray the Lord of the harvest to send out laborers into His harvest.

[22-A]   A disciple is not above his teacher, nor a servant above his master. It is enough for a disciple that he be like his teacher, and a servant like his master. If they have called the master of the house Beelzebub, how much more will they call those of his household! Therefore do not fear them. For there is nothing covered that will not be revealed, and hidden that will not be known.

[23-A]   He who receives you receives Me, and he who receives Me receives Him who sent Me. He who receives a prophet in the name of a prophet shall receive a prophet's reward. And he who receives a righteous man in the name of a righteous man shall receive a righteous man's reward. And whoever gives one of these little ones only a cup of cold water in the name of a disciple, assuredly, I say to you, he shall by no means lose his reward.

[24-A]   Assuredly, I say to you, among those born of women there has not risen one greater than John the Baptist; but he who is least in the kingdom of heaven is greater than he.

[25-A]   Who is My mother and who are My brothers? *And he stretched out His hand toward His disciples and said*, Here are My mother and My brothers! For whoever does the will of My Father in heaven is My brother and sister and mother.

[26-A]   For the hearts of this people have grown dull. Their ears are hard of hearing, and their eyes they have closed, lest they should see with their eyes and hear with their ears, lest they should understand with their hearts and turn, so that I should heal them. But blessed are your eyes for they see, and your ears for they hear; for assuredly, I say to you that many prophets and righteous men desired to see what you see, and did not see it, and to hear what you hear, and did not hear it.

[27-A]   When it is evening you say, 'It will be fair weather, for the sky is red'; and in the morning, 'It will be foul weather today, for the sky is red and threatening.' Hypocrites! You know how to discern the face of the sky, but you cannot discern the signs of the times.

[28-A]   *Then Jesus said to His disciples*, If anyone desires to come after Me, let him deny himself, and take up his cross, and follow Me. For whoever desires to save his life will lose it, but whoever loses his life for My sake will find it.

[29-A]   For assuredly, I say to you, if you have faith as a mustard seed, you will say to this mountain, 'Move from here to there,' and it will move; and nothing will be impossible for you.

[30-A]   Assuredly, I say to you, unless you are converted and become as little children, you will by no means enter the kingdom of heaven. Therefore whoever humbles himself as this little child is the greatest in the kingdom of heaven. Whoever receives one little child like this in My name receives Me. But whoever causes one of these little ones who believe in Me to sin, it would be better for him if a millstone were hung around his neck, and he were drowned in the depth of the sea.

[31–A]   Again I say to you that if two of you agree on earth concerning anything that they ask, it will be done for them by My Father in heaven.

[32–A]   Have you not read that He who made them at the beginning 'made them male and female,' and said, 'For this reason a man shall leave his father and mother and be joined to his wife, and the two shall become one flesh'? So then, they are no longer two but one flesh. Therefore what God has joined together, let not man separate.

[33–A]   *Then little children were brought to Him that He might put His hands on them and pray, but the disciples rebuked them. But Jesus said,* Let the little children come to Me, and do not forbid them; for of such is the kingdom of heaven.

[34–A]   Why do you call Me good? No one is good but One, that is, God. But if you want to enter into life, keep the commandments.

[35–A]   Assuredly I say to you, that in the regeneration, when the Son of Man sits on the throne of His glory, you who have followed Me will also sit on twelve thrones, judging the twelve tribes of Israel. And everyone who has left houses or brothers or sisters or father or mother or wife or children or lands, for My name's sake, shall receive a hundredfold, and inherit eternal life. But many who are first will be last, and the last first.

[36–A]   You know that the rulers of the Gentiles lord it over them, and those who are great exercise authority over them. Yet it shall not be so among you; but whoever desires to become great among you, let him be your servant. And whoever desires to be first among you, let him be your slave — just as the Son of Man did not come to be served, but to serve, and to give His life a ransom for many.

[37-A]   It is written, 'My house shall be called a house of prayer,' but you have made it a 'den of thieves.'

[38-A]   And whatever things you ask in prayer, believing, you will receive.

[39-A]   Render therefore to Caesar the things that are Caesar's, and to God the things that are God's.

[40-A]   But concerning the resurrection of the dead, have you not read what was spoken to you by God, saying, 'I am the God of Abraham, the God of Isaac, and the God of Jacob'? God is not the God of the dead, but of the living.

[41-A]   *Then Jesus spoke to the multitudes and to His disciples, saying*: The scribes and the Pharisees sit in Moses' seat. Therefore whatever they tell you to observe, that observe and do, but do not do according to their works; for they say, and do not do. For they bind heavy burdens, hard to bear, and lay them on men's shoulders; but they themselves will not move them with one of their fingers.

[42-B]   *Then Jesus said to them*, Follow Me, and I will make you become fishers of men.

[43-B]   The sabbath was made for man, not man for the sabbath; so the Son of man is lord even of the sabbath.

[44–B]   Then are you also without understanding? Do you not see that whatever goes into a man from outside cannot defile him, since it enters, not his heart but his stomach, and so passess on? (*Thus he declared all foods clean.*) *And he said,* What comes out of a man is what defiles a man. For from within, out of the heart of man, come evil thoughts, fornication, theft, murder, adultery, coveting, wickedness, deceit, licentiousness, envy, slander, pride, foolishness. All these evil things come from within, and they defile a man.

[45–B]   If any man would come after me, let him deny himself and take up his cross and follow me. For whoever would save his life will lose it; and whoever loses his life for my sake and the gospel's will save it.

[46–B]   For whoever is ashamed of me and my words in this adulterous and sinful generation, of him will the Son of man also be ashamed, when he comes in the glory of his Father with the holy angels.

[47–B]   Truly, I say to you, there are some standing here who will not taste death before they see that the Kingdom of God has come with power.

[48–B]   Whoever receives one such child in my name receives me; and whoever receives me, receives not me but him who sent me.

[49–B]   *And they were exceedingly astonished, and said to him, 'Then who can be saved?' Jesus looked at them and said,* With men it is impossible, but not with God; for all things are possible with God.

[50–B]   Truly, I say to you, there is no one who has left house or brothers or sisters or mother or father or children or lands, for my sake and for the gospel, who will not recieve a hundredfold now in this time, houses and brothers and sisters and mothers and children and lands, with persecutions, and in the age to come eternal life. But many that are first will be last, and the last first.

[51-B]   Have faith in God.

[52-B]   Truly, I say to you, whoever says to this mountain, 'Be taken up and cast into the sea,' and does not doubt in his heart, but believes that what he says will come to pass, it will be done for him.

[53-B]   Therefore I tell you, whatever you ask in prayer, believe that you have received it, and it will be yours. And whenever you stand praying, forgive, if you have anything against any one; so that your Father also who is in heaven may forgive you your trespasses.

[54-B]   Is not this why you are wrong, that you know neither the scriptures nor the power of God? For when they rise from the dead, they neither marry nor are given in marriage, but are like angels in heaven.

[55-B]   Beware of the scribes, who like to go about in long robes, and to have salutations in the market places and the best seats in the synagogues and the places of honor at feasts, who devour widows' houses and for a pretense make long prayers. They will receive the greater condemnation.

[56-B]   *And he sat down opposite the treasury, and watched the multitude putting money into the treasury. Many rich people put in large sums. And a poor widow came, and put in two copper coins, which make a penny. And he called his disciples to him, and said to them,* Truly, I say to you, this poor widow has put in more than all those who are contributing to the treasury. For they all contributed out of their abundance; but she out of her poverty has put in everything she had, her whole living.

[57-B]   He who believes and is baptized will be saved; but he who does not believe will be condemned. And these signs will accompany those who believe: in my name they will cast out demons; they will speak in new tongues; they will pick up serpents, and if they drink any deadly thing, it will not hurt them; they will lay their hands on the sick, and they will recover.

[58-C]   It is written, 'Man shall not live by bread alone, but by every word of God.'

[59-C]   It has been said, 'You shall not tempt the Lord your God.'

[60-C]   The Spirit of the Lord is upon Me, because He has anointed me to preach the gospel to the poor; he has sent Me to heal the brokenhearted, to proclaim liberty to the captives and recovery of sight to the blind, to set at liberty those who are oppressed; to proclaim the acceptable year of the Lord.

[61-C]   *When the messengers of John had departed, He began to speak to the multitudes concerning John*: What did you go out into the wilderness to see? A reed shaken by the wind? But what did you go out to see? A man clothed in soft garments? Indeed those who are gorgeously appareled and live in luxury are in kings' courts. But what did you go out to see? A prophet? Yes, I say to you, and more than a prophet.

This is he of whom it is written: 'Behold, I send My messenger before Your face, who will prepare Your way before You.' For I say to you, among those born of women there is not a greater prophet than John the Baptist; but he who is least in the kingdom of God is greater than he.

[62–C]   Your faith has saved you. Go in peace.

[63–C]   My mother and My brothers are these who hear the word of God and do it.

[64–C]   Where is your faith?

[65–C]   The harvest truly is great, but the laborers are few; therefore pray the Lord of the harvest to send out laborers into His harvest.

[66–C]   Behold, I give you the authority to trample on serpents and scorpions, and over all the power of the enemy, and nothing shall by any means hurt you. Nevertheless do not rejoice in this, that the spirits are subject to you, but rather rejoice because your names are written in heaven.

[67–C]   Blessed are the eyes which see the things you see; for I tell you that many prophets and kings have desired to see what you see, and have not seen it, and to hear what you hear, and have not heard it.

[68–C]   So I say to you, ask, and it will be given to you; seek, and you will find; knock, and it will be opened to you. For everyone who asks receives, and he who seeks finds, and to him who knocks it will be opened.

[69–C]   If a son asks for bread of any father among you, will he give him a stone? Or if he asks for a fish, will he give him a serpent instead of a fish? Or if he asks for an egg, will he offer him a scorpion? If you then, being evil, know how to give good gifts to your children, how much more will your heavenly Father give the Holy Spirit to those who ask Him!

[70–C]   Every kingdom divided against itself is brought to desolation, and a house divided against a house falls.

[71–C]   When a strong man, fully armed, guards his own palace, his goods are in peace. But when a stronger than he comes upon him and overcomes him, he takes from him all his armor in which he trusted, and divides his spoils.

[72–C]   More than that, blessed are those who hear the word of God and keep it!

[73–C]   Man, who made Me a judge or an arbitrator over you?

[74–C]   Nevertheless I must journey today, tomorrow, and the day following; for it cannot be that a prophet should perish outside of Jerusalem.

[75–C]   O Jerusalem, Jerusalem, the one who kills the prophets and stones those who are sent to her! How often I wanted to gather your children together, as a hen gathers her brood under her wings, but you were not willing! See! Your house is left to you desolate; and assuredly, I say to you, you shall not see Me until the time comes when you say, 'Blessed is He who comes in the name of the Lord!'

[76–C]   Which of you, having a donkey or an ox that has fallen into a pit, will not immediately pull him out on the Sabbath day?

[77–C]   And I say to you, make friends for yourselves by unrighteous mammon, that when you fail, they may receive you into an everlasting home. He who is faithful in what is least is faithful also in much; and he who is unjust in what is least is unjust also in much. Therefore if you have not been faithful in the unrighteous mammon, who will commit to your trust the true riches? And if you have not been faithful in what is another man's, who will give you what is your own?

[78–C]   You are those who justify yourselves before men, but God knows your hearts. For what is highly esteemed among men is an abomination in the sight of God.

[79–C]   The law and the prophets were until John. Since that time the kingdom of God has been preached, and everyone is pressing into it.

[80–C]   Whoever divorces his wife and marries another commits adultery; and whoever marries her who is divorced from her husband commits adultery.

[81–C]   If you have faith as a mustard seed, you can say to this mulberry tree, 'Be pulled up by the roots and be planted in the sea,' and it would obey you.

[82–C]   The kingdom of God does not come with observation; nor will they say, 'See here!' or 'See there!' For indeed, the kingdom of God is within you.

[83–C]   For as the lightning that flashes out of one part under heaven shines to the other part under heaven, so also the Son of Man will be in His day. But first he must suffer many things and be rejected by this generation.

[84–C]   The things which are impossible with men are possible with God.

[85–C]   . . . for the Son of Man has come to seek and to save that which was lost.

[86–C]   If you had known, even you, especially in this your day, the things that make for your peace! But now they are hidden from your eyes. For days will come upon you when your enemies will build an embankment around you, surround you and close you in on every side, and level you, and your children within you, to the ground; and they will not leave in you one stone upon another, because you did not know the time of your visitation.

[87–C]   The sons of this age marry and are given in marriage. But those who are counted worthy to attain that age, and the resurrection from the dead, neither marry nor are given in marriage; nor can they die anymore, for they are equal to the angels and are sons of God, being sons of the resurrection.

[88–C]   But even Moses showed in the burning bush passage that the dead are raised, when he called the Lord 'the God of Abraham, the God of Isaac, and the God of Jacob.' For He is not the God of the dead but of the living, for all live to Him.

[89–C]   Behold, I send the Promise of My Father upon you; but tarry in the city of Jerusalem until you are endued with power from on high.

[90–D]   Truly, truly, I say to you, you will see heaven opened, and the angels of God ascending and descending upon the Son of man.

[91–D]   Truly, truly, I say to you, unless one is born anew, he cannot see the kingdom of God.

[92–D]   Truly, truly, I say to you, unless one is born of water and the Spirit, he cannot enter the kingdom of God. That which is born of the flesh is flesh, and that which is born of the Spirit is spirit. Do not marvel that I said to you, 'You must be born anew.' The wind blows where it wills, and you hear the sound of it, but you do not know whence it comes or whither it goes; so it is with every one who is born of the Spirit.

[93–D]   Truly, truly, I say to you, we speak of what we know, and bear witness to what we have seen; but you do not receive our testimony. If I have told you earthly things and you do not believe, how can you believe if I tell you heavenly things? No one has ascended into heaven but he who descended from heaven, the Son of man.

[94–D]   And this is the judgment, that the light has come into the world, and men loved darkness rather than light, because their deeds were evil. For every one who does evil hates the light, and does not come to the light, lest his deeds should be exposed. But he who does what is true comes to the light, that it may be clearly seen that his deeds have been wrought in God.

[95–D]   *Jesus said to her*, Woman, believe me, the hour is coming when neither on this mountain nor in Jerusalem will you worship the Father.

[96–D]   You worship what you do not know; we worship what we know, for salvation is from the Jews. But the hour is coming, and now is, when the true worshipers will worship the Father in spirit and truth, for such the Father seeks to worship him. God is spirit, and those who worship him must worship in spirit and truth.

[97–D]   Do you not say, 'There are yet four months, then comes the harvest'? I tell you, lift up your eyes, and see how the fields are already white for harvest. He who reaps receives wages, and gathers fruit for eternal life, so that sower and reaper may rejoice together. For here the saying holds true, 'One sows and another reaps.' I sent you to reap that for which you did not labor; others have labored, and you have entered into their labor.

[98–D]   *Jesus then said to them,* Truly, truly, I say to you, it was not Moses who gave you the bread from heaven; my Father gives you the true bread from heaven. For the bread of God is that which comes down from heaven, and gives life to the world.

[99–D]   No one can come to me unless the Father who sent me draws him; and I will raise him up at the last day. It is written in the prophets, 'And they shall all be taught by God.' Every one who has heard and learned from the Father comes to me. Not that any one has seen the Father except him who is from God; he has seen the Father.

[100–D]   As the living Father sent me, and I live because of the Father, so he who eats me will live because of me. This is the bread which came down from heaven, not such as the fathers ate and died; he who eats this bread will live forever.

[101–D]   Then what if you were to see the Son of man ascending where he was before? It is the spirit that gives life, the flesh is of no avail; the words that I have spoken to you are spirit and life. But there are some of you that do not believe.

[102-D] *Jesus said to them,* My time has not yet come, but your time is always here.

[103-D] He who speaks on his own authority seeks his own glory; but he who seeks the glory of him who sent him is true, and in him there is no falsehood. Did not Moses give you the law? Yet none of you keeps the law. Why do you seek to kill me?

[104-D] *On the last day of the feast, the great day, Jesus stood up and proclaimed,* If any one thirst, let him come to me and drink. He who believes in me, as the scripture has said, 'Out of his heart shall flow rivers of living water.'

[105-D] Truly, truly, I say to you, every one who commits sin is a slave to sin. The slave does not continue in the house for ever; the son continues for ever. So if the Son makes you free, you will be free indeed.

[106-D] I speak of what I have seen with my Father, and you do what you have heard from your father.

[107-D] *Jesus said to them,* If God were your Father, you would love me, for I proceeded and came forth from God; I came not of my own accord, but he sent me. Why do you not understand what I say? It is because you cannot bear to hear my word.

[108-D] You are of your father the devil, and your will is to do your father's desires. He was a murderer from the beginning, and has nothing to do with the truth, because there is no truth in him. When he lies, he speaks according to his own nature, for he is a liar and the father of lies. But, because I tell the truth, you do not believe me. Which of you convicts me of sin? If I tell the truth, why do you not believe me?

[109-D] He who is of God hears the words of God; the reason why you do not hear them is that you are not of God.

[110-D] Are there not twelve hours in the day? If any one walks in the day, he does not stumble, because he sees the light of this world. But if any one walks in the night, he stumbles, because the light is not in him.

[111-D] I am the resurrection and the life; he who believes in me, though he die, yet shall he live, and whoever lives and believes in me shall never die. Do you believe this?

[112-D] Now is the judgment of this world, now shall the ruler of this world be cast out.

[113-D] By this all men will know that you are my disciples, if you have love for one another.

[114-D] Let not your hearts be troubled; believe in God, believe also in me. In my Father's house are many rooms; if it were not so, would I have told you that I go to prepare a place for you? And when I go and prepare a place for you, I will come again and will take you to myself; that where I am you may be also.

[115-D] He who has my commandments and keeps them, he it is who loves me; and he who loves me will be loved by my Father, and I will love him and manifest myself to him.

[116-D] If a man loves me, he will keep my word, and my Father will love him, and we will come to him and make our home with him. He who does not love me does not keep my words; and the word which you hear is not mine but the Father's who sent me. These things have I spoken to you, while I am still with you.

[117-D]   You did not choose me, but I chose you and appointed you that you should go and bear fruit and that your fruit should abide; so that whatever you ask the Father in my name, he may give it to you.

[118-D]   If the world hates you, know that it has hated me before it hated you. If you were of the world, the world would love its own; but because you are not of the world, but I chose you out of the world, therefore the world hates you.

[119-D]   He who hates me hates my Father also.

[120-D]   But when the Counselor comes, whom I shall send to you from the Father, even the Spirit of truth, who proceeds from the Father, he will bear witness to me; and you also are witnesses, because you have been with me from the beginning.

[121-D]   Hitherto you have asked nothing in my name; ask, and you will receive, that your joy may be full.

[122-D]   The hour is coming, indeed it has come, when you will be scattered, every man to his home, and will leave me alone; yet I am not alone, for the Father is with me. I have said this to you, that in me you may have peace. In the world you have tribulation; but be of good cheer, I have overcome the world.

[123-F]   *Jesus said,* Let him who seeks continue seeking until he finds. When he finds, he will become troubled. When he becomes troubled, he will be astonished, and he will rule over the all.

[124-F] *Jesus said,* The man old in days will not hesitate to ask a small child seven days old about the place of life, and he will live. For many who are first will become last, and they will become one and the same.

[125-F] *Jesus said,* Recognize what is in your sight, and that which is hidden from you will become plain to you. For there is nothing hidden which will not become manifest.

[126-F] *Jesus said,* Blessed is the lion which becomes man when consumed by man; and cursed is the man whom the lion consumes, and the lion becomes man.

[127-F] *Jesus said,* This heaven will pass away, and the one above it will pass away. The dead are not alive, and the living will not die. In the days when you consumed what is dead, you made it what is alive. When you come to dwell in the light, what will you do? On the day when you were one you became two. But when you become two, what will you do?

[128-F] *Jesus said,* Blessed is he who came into being before he came into being. If you become my disciples and listen to my words, these stones will minister to you. For there are five trees for you in Paradise which remain undisturbed summer and winter and whose leaves do not fall. Whoever becomes acquainted with them will not experience death.

[129-F] *Jesus saw infants being suckled. He said to his disciples,* These infants being suckled are like those who enter the Kingdom.
 They said to Him, 'Shall we then, as children, enter the Kingdom?'
 Jesus said to them, When you make the two one, and when you make the inside like the outside and the outside like the inside, and

the above like the below, and when you make the male and the fe-male one and the same, so that the male not be male nor the female female; and when you fashion eyes in place of an eye, and a hand in place of a hand, and a foot in place of a foot, and a likeness in place of a likeness; then will you enter the Kingdom.

[130–F]   *Jesus said,* I shall choose you, one out of a thousand, and two out of ten thousand, and they shall stand as a single one.

[131–F]   *His disciples said to him, 'Show us the place where you are, since it is necessary for us to seek it.'*
   He said to them, Whoever has ears, let him hear. There is light within a man of light, and he lights up the whole world. If he does not shine, he is in darkness.

[132–F]   *Jesus said,* You see the mote in your brother's eye, but you do not see the beam in your own eye. When you cast the beam out of your own eye, then you will see clearly to cast the mote from your brother's eye.

[133–F]   *Jesus said,* If the flesh came into being because of spirit, it is a wonder. But if spirit came into being because of the body, it is a wonder of wonders. Indeed, I am amazed at how this great wealth has made its home in this poverty.

[134–F]   *Jesus said,* A city being built on a high mountain and forti-fied cannot fall, nor can it be hidden.

[135–F]   *Jesus said,* If a blind man leads a blind man, they will both fall into a pit.

[136–F]   *His disciples said, 'When will you become revealed to us and when shall we see you?' Jesus said,* When you disrobe without being ashamed and take up your garments and place them under your feet like little children and tread on them, then will you see the Son of the Living One, and you will not be afraid.

[137-F] *Jesus said,* The Pharisees and the scribes have taken the keys of Knowledge and hidden them. They themselves have not entered, nor have they allowed to enter those who wish to. You, however, be as wise as serpents and as innocent as doves.

[138-F] *Jesus said,* Whoever has something in his hand will receive more, and whoever has nothing will be deprived of even the little he has.

[139-F] *Jesus said,* Become passers-by.

[140-F] *Jesus said,* Among those born of women, from Adam until John the Baptist, there is no one so superior to John the Baptist that his eyes should not be lowered before him. Yet I have said, whichever one of you comes to be a child will be acquainted with the Kingdom and will become superior to John.

[141-F] *Jesus said,* If two make peace with each other in this one house, they will say to the mountain, 'Move away,' and it will move away.

[142-F] *Jesus said,* Blessed are the solitary and the elect, for you will find the Kingdom. For you are from it, and to it you will return.

[143-F] *Jesus said,* If they say to you, 'Where did you come from?', say to them, 'We came from the light, the place where the light came into being on its own accord and established itself and became manifest through their image.' If they say to you, 'Is it you?', say, 'We are its children, and we are the elect of the Living Father.' If they ask you, 'What is the sign of your Father in you?', say to them, 'It is movement and repose.'

[144–F]   *His disciples said to him, 'When will the repose of the dead come about, and when will the new world come?'*

He said to them, What you look forward to has already come, but you do not recognize it.

[145–F]   *His disciples said to him, 'Is circumcision beneficial or not?'*

He said to them, If it were beneficial, their father would beget them already circumcised from their mother. Rather, the true circumcision in spirit has become completely profitable.

[146–F]   *Jesus said,* Blessed are the poor, for yours is the Kingdom of Heaven.

[147–F]   *Jesus said,* Whoever does not hate his father and his mother cannot become a discile to me. And whoever does not hate his brothers and sisters and take up his cross in My way will not be worthy of Me.

[148–F]   *Jesus said,* Whoever has come to understand the world has found only a corpse, and whoever has found a corpse is superior to the world.

[149–F]   *Jesus said,* Blessed is the man who has suffered and found life.

[150–F]   *Jesus said,* Take heed of the Living One while you are alive, lest you die and seek to see Him and be unable to do so.

[151-F] *Jesus said*, Show me the stone which the builders have rejected. That one is the cornerstone.

[152-F] *Jesus said*, Whoever believes that the All itself is deficient is himself completely deficient.

[153-F] *Jesus said*, Blessed are you when you are hated and persecuted. Wherever you have been persucuted they will find no Place.

[154-F] *Jesus said*, Blessed are they who have been persecuted within themselves. It is they who have truly come to know the Father. Blessed are the hungry, for the belly of him who desires will be filled.

[155-F] *A man said to him, 'Tell my brothers to divide my father's possessions with me.'*
He said to him, O man, who has made me a divider? *He turned to his disciples and said to them*, I am not a divider, am I?

[156-F] *Jesus said*, The harvest is great but the laborers are few. Beseech the Lord, therefore, to send out laborers to the harvest.

[157-F] *He said*, O Lord, there are many around the drinking trough, but there is nothing in the cistern.

[158-F] *Jesus said*, Why have you come out into the desert? To see a reed shaken by the wind? And to see a man clothed in fine garments like your kings and your great men? Upon them are the fine garments, and they are unable to discern the truth.

[159-F] *Jesus said*, He who has recognized the world has found the body, but he who has found the body is superior to the world.

[160–F]   *Jesus said,* Let him who has grown rich be king, and let him who possesses power renounce it.

[161–F]   *Jesus said,* The images are manifest to man, but the light in them remains concealed in the image of the light of the Father. He will become manifest, but his image will remain concealed by his light.

[162–F]   *Jesus said,* When you see your likeness, you rejoice. But when you see your images which came into being before you, and which neither die nor become manifest, how much you will have to bear!

[163–F]   *Jesus said,* Adam came into being from a great power and a great wealth, but he did not become worthy of you. For had he been worthy, he would not have experienced death.

[164–F]   *Jesus said,* The angels and the prophets will come to you and give to you those things you already have. And you too, give them those things which you have, and say to yourselves, 'When will they come and take what is theirs?'

[165–F]   *They said to Him, 'Tell us who You are so that we may believe in you.' He said to them,* You read the face of the sky and of the earth, but you have not recognized the one who is before you, and you do not know how to read this moment.

[166–F]   *Jesus said,* Seek and you will find. Yet, what you asked Me about in former times and which I did not tell you then, now I do desire to tell, but you do not inquire after it.

[167–F]   *Jesus said,* He who seeks will find, and he who knocks will be let in.

[168-F]   *The disciples said to Him, 'Your brothers and Your mother are standing outside.'*

He said to them, Those here who do the will of My Father are My brothers and My mother. It is they who will enter the Kingdom of My Father.

[169-F]   *They showed Jesus a gold coin and said to Him, 'Caesar's men demand taxes from us.'*

He said to them, Give Caesar what belongs to Caesar, give God what belongs to God, and give Me what is Mine.

[170-F]   *Jesus said,* Whoever does not hate his father and his mother as I do cannot become a disciple to Me. And whoever does not love his father and his mother as I do cannot become a disciple to me. For My mother gave me falsehood, but My true Mother gave me life.

[171-F]   *Jesus said,* He who knows the father and the mother will be called the son of a harlot.

[172-F]   *Jesus said,* When you make the two one, you will become the sons of man, and when you say, 'Mountain, move away,' it will move away.

[173-F]   *Jesus said,* Whoever finds the world and becomes rich, let him renounce the world.

[174-F]   *Simon Peter said to them, 'Let Mary leave us, for women are not worthy of Life.'*

Jesus said, I myself shall lead her in order to make her male, so that she too may become a living spirit resembling you males. For every woman who will make herself male will enter the Kingdom of Heaven.

[175-G]   Verily I say unto to you, no one will ever enter the kingdom of heaven at my bidding, but only because you yourselves are full.

[176-G]   *The Savior said,* You have received mercy. Do you not, then, desire to be filled? And your heart is drunken; do you not, then, desire to be sober? Therefore be ashamed! Henceforth, waking or sleeping, remember that you have seen the Son of Man, and spoken with him in person, and listened to him in person.

[177-G]   *Then I asked him, 'Lord, how shall we be able to prophesy to those who request us to prophesy to them? For there are many who ask us, and look to us to hear an oracle from us.' The Lord answered and said,* Do you not know that the head of prophecy was cut off with John?

[178-G]   Come to hate hypocrisy and the evil thought; for it is the thought that gives birth to hypocrisy; but hypocrisy is far from truth.

[179-G]   Therefore I say to you, be sober; do not be deceived!

[180-G]   And I have commanded you to follow me, and I have taught you what to say before the archons. Observe that I have descended and have spoken and undergone tribulation and carried off my crown after saving you. For I came down to dwell with you so that you in turn might dwell with me. And, finding your houses unceiled, I have made my abode in the houses that could receive me at the time of my descent.

[181-G]   I remembered your tears and your mourning and your anguish; they are far behind us. But now, you who are outside of the Father's inheritance, weep where it is necessary, and mourn and preach what is good, as the Son is ascending as he should. Verily I say unto you, had I been sent to those who listen to me, and had I spoken with them, I would never have come down to earth. So, then, be ashamed before them now!

[182-G] This is why I say to you, for your sakes I came down. You are the beloved; you are they who will be the cause of life in many. Invoke the Father, implore God often, and he will give to you. Blessed is he who has seen you with Him when He was proclaimed among the angels, and glorified among the saints; yours is life. Rejoice and be glad as sons of God. Keep his will that you may be saved; accept reproof from me and save yourselves. I intercede on your behalf with the Father, and he will forgive you much.

[183-G] Do not make the kingdom of heaven a desert within you. Do not be proud because of the light that illumines, but be to yourselves as I myself am to you. For your sakes I have placed myself under the curse, that you may be saved.

[184-G] . . . and when you are elated at the promise of life, are you yet sad, and do you grieve when you are instructed in the kingdom? But you, through faith and knowledge, have received life. Therefore disdain the rejection when you hear it, but when you hear the promise, rejoice the more. Verily I say unto you, he who will receive life and believe in the kingdom will never leave it, not even if the Father wishes to banish him.

[185-G] . . . blessed are they who have proclaimed the Son before his descent that, when I have come, I might ascend again. Thrice blessed are they who were proclaimed by the Son before they came to be, that you might have a portion among them.

[186–H]   *The Lord said to the disciples,* Bring out from every other house. Bring into the house of the Father. But do not take anything in the house of the Father nor carry it off.

[187–H]   Ask your mother and she will give you of the things which are another's.

[188–H]   *The Lord went into the dye works of Levi. He took seventy-two different colors and threw them into the vat. He took them out all white. And he said,* Even so has the Son of Man come as a dyer.

[189–H]   *The Lord said,* Blessed is he who is before he came into being. For he who is, has been and shall be.

[190–H]   *The Lord said,* I came to make the things below like the things above, and the things outside like those inside. I came to unite them in that place.

[191–H]   Go into your chamber and shut the door behind you, and pray to your Father who is in secret.

[192–H]   Thus we should fulfill all righteousness.

[193–H]   *The Lord said it well:* Some have entered the kingdom of heaven laughing and they have come out.

[194–H]   He who sins is the slave of sin.

[195–H]   Love builds up.

[196–H]   Love covers a multitude of sins.

[197–H]   Already the ax is laid at the root of the trees.

[198–I]   If the things that are visible to you are obscure to you, how can you hear about the things that are not visible? If the deeds of the truth that are visible in the world are difficult for you to perform, how indeed, then, shall you perform those that pertain to the exalted height and to the Pleroma which are not visible? And how shall you be called 'laborers'? In this respect you are apprentices, and have not yet received the height of perfection.

[199–I]   *The Savior said,* All bodies of men and beasts are begotten irrational. Surely it is evident in the way a creature . . . Those, however, that are above are not visible among things that are visible, but are visible in their own root, and it is their fruit that nourishes them. But these visible bodies eat of creatures similar to them with the result that the bodies change. Now that which changes will decay and perish, and has no hope of life from then on, since that body is bestial. So just as the body of the beasts perishes, so also will these formations perish. Do they not derive from intercourse like that of the beasts? If the body too derives from intercourse, how will it beget anything different from beasts? So, therefore, you are babes until you become perfect.

[200–I]   *Jesus said,* It is in light that light exists.

[202–I]   *The Savior said,* O Blessed Thomas, of course this visible light shone on your behalf — not in order that you remain here, but rather that you come forth — and whenever all the elect abandon bestiality, then this light will withdraw up to its essence, and its essence will welcome it since it is a good servant.

[202–I]   Truly, as for those, do not esteem them as men, but regard them as beasts, for just as beasts devour one another, so also men of this sort devour one another. On the contrary, they are deprived of the kingdom since they love the sweetness of the fire and are servants of death and rush to the works of corruption. They fulfill the lust of their fathers. They will be thrown down to the abyss and be afflicted by the torment of the bitterness of their evil nature. For they will be scourged so as to make them rush headlong to the place that they do not know, and they will not recede from their limbs patiently, but with despair. And they rejoice over the concern for this life with madness and derangement! Some pursue this derangement without realizing their madness, thinking that they are wise. They are beguiled by the beauty of their body as if it would not perish. And they are frenetic; their thought is occupied with their deeds. But it is the fire that will burn them!

[203-I]   *The Savior replied*, Listen to what I am going to tell you and believe in the truth. That which sows and that which is sown will dissolve in their fire — within the fire and water — and they will hide in tombs of darkness. And after a long time they shall appear as the fruit of the evil trees, being punished, being slain in the mouth of beasts and men at the instigation of the rains and winds and air and the light that shines above.

[204-I]   Blessed are you who have prior knowledge of the stumbling blocks and who flee alien things.

[205-I]   Blessed are you who are reviled and not esteemed on account of the love their Lord has for them.

[206-I]   Blessed are you who weep and are oppressed by those without hope, for you will be released from every bondage.

[207-I]   Watch and pray that you not come to be in the flesh, but rather that you come forth from the bondage of the bitterness of this life. And as you pray, you will find rest, for you have left behind the suffering and the disgrace. For when you come forth from the sufferings and passion of the body, you will receive rest from the Good One, and you will reign with the King, you joined with him and he with you, from now on, forever and ever. Amen.

[208-J]   Peter, blessed are those above belonging to the Father who revealed life to those who are from the life, through me, since I reminded them, they who are built on what is strong, that they may hear my word and distinguish words of unrighteousness and transgression of law from righteousness, as being from the height of every word of this pleroma of truth, having been enlightened in good pleasure by him whom the principalities sought. But they did not find him, nor was he mentioned among any generation of the prophets. He has now appeared among these, in him who appeared, who is the Son of Man who is exalted above the heavens in a fear of men of like essence. But you yourself, Peter, become perfect in accordance with your name with myself, the one who chose you, because from you I have established a base for the remnant whom I have summoned to knowledge. Therefore be strong until the imitation of righteousness — of him who had summoned you, having summoned you to know him in a way which is worth doing because of the rejection which happened to him, and the sinews of his hands and his feet, and the crowning by those of the middle region, and the body of his radiance which they bring in hope of service because of a reward of honor — as he was about to reprove you three times in this night.

[209-J]   Peter, I have told you many times that they are blind ones who have no guide.

[210-J]   For evil cannot produce good fruit. For the place from which each of them is produces that which is like itself; for not every soul is of the truth, nor of immortality. For every soul of these ages has death assigned to it in our view, because it is always a slave, since it is created for its desires and their eternal destruction, in which they are and from which they are. They (the souls) love the creatures of the matter which came forth with them. But the immortal souls are not like these, O Peter. But indeed, as long as the hour is not yet come, the immortal soul shall resemble a mortal one. But it shall not reveal its nature, that it alone is the immortal one, and thinks about immortality, having faith, and desiring to renounce these things.

[211-J]   Therefore all that which exists not will dissolve into what exists not. For deaf and blind ones join only with their own kind. But others shall change from evil words and misleading mysteries. Some who do not understand mystery speak of things which they do not understand, but they will boast that the mystery of the truth is theirs alone. And in haughtiness they shall grasp at pride to envy the immortal soul which has become a pledge. For every authority, rule, and power of the aeons wishes to be with these in the creation of the world, in order that those who are not, having been forgotten by those that are, may praise them, though they have not been saved, nor have they been brought to the Way by them, always wishing that they may become imperishable ones. For if the immortal soul receives power in an intellectual spirit . . . But immediately they join with one of those who misled them.

[212-J]   And there shall be others of those who are outside our number who name themselves bishop and also deacons, as if they have received their authority from God. They bend themselves under the judgment of the leaders. Those people are dry canals.

[213-J]   *The Savior said*, For a time determined for them in proportion to their error they will rule over the little ones. And after the completion of the error, the never-aging one of the immortal understanding shall become young, and they (the little ones) shall rule over those who are their rulers. The root of their error he shall pluck out, and he shall put it to shame so that it shall be manifest in all the impudence which it has assumed to itself. And such ones shall become unchangeable, O Peter.

[214-J]   These things, then, which you saw you shall present to those of another race who are not of this age. For there will be no honor in any man who is not immortal, but only in those who were chosen from an immortal substance, which has shown that it is able to contain him who gives his abundance. Therefore I said, 'Every one who has, it will be given to him, and he will have plenty.' But he who does not have, that is, the man of this place, who is completely dead, who is removed from the planting of the creation of what is begotten, whom, if one of the immortal essence appears, they think that they possess him — it will be taken from him and be added to the one who is. You, therefore, be courageous and do not fear at all. For I shall be with you in order that none of your enemies may prevail over you. Peace be to you. Be strong!

[215-K]   *The Savior said*, All natures, all formations, all creatures exist in and with one another, and they will be resolved again into their own roots. For the nature of matter is resolved into the roots of its nature alone. He who has ears to hear, let him hear.

[216-K]   *The Savior said*, There is no sin, but it is you who make sin when you do the things that are like the nature of adultery, which is called 'sin.' That is why the Good came into your midst, to the essence of every nature, in order to restore it to its root.

[217–K]   Blessed are you, that you did not waver at the sight of me. For where the mind is, there is the treasure.

[218–L]   *Therefore the savior cries out,* No one can come to me unless my Father draws him and brings him to me; and I myself will raise him up on the last day.

[219–L]   *Again the Savior said,* Blessed are those who mourn, for it is they who will be pitied; blessed, those who are hungry, for it is they who will be filled.

[220–L]   If one does not hate his soul he cannot follow me.

[221–M]   *The Savior said to his disciples,* Already the time has come, brothers, that we should leave behind our labor and stand in the rest; for he who stands in the rest will rest forever.

[222–M]   *The Lord said,* The one who seeks is also the one who reveals.

[223–M]   *The Lord said,* The one who speaks is also the one who hears, and the one who sees is also the one who reveals.

[224–M]   *The Lord said,* He who is from the truth does not die; he who is from the woman dies.

[225–M]   *The Lord said,* When you leave behind you the things that will not be able to follow you, then you will put yourselves to rest.

[226–M]   *The Lord said,* Whoever seeks life knows this, for this is their wealth. For the enjoyment of this world is a lie, and its gold and its silver is error.

[227–M]   *He said,* Love and goodness.

[228–M]   *The Lord said,* Pray in the place where there is no woman.

[229–N]   *And he said,* Peace to you! My Peace I give to you!

[230–N]   *The Savior said to them,* I desire that you know that all men born on earth from the foundation of the world until now are dust. Inquiring about God, who he is, and what he is like, they have not found him. Now the wisest among them have speculated on the basis of the ordering of the world and its movement. But their speculation has not reached the truth. For the ordering is said to be directed in three ways by all the philosophers, and hence they do not agree. For some of them say about the world that it is directed by itself. Some, that it is providence that directs it. Some, that it is fate. Now, it is none of these. Again, of the three opinions that I have just described, none is close to the truth, and they are from man. But I, who came from the boundless Light, I am here. For I am he who knows it (the Light), so that I might speak to you concerning the precise nature of the truth. For whatever is from itself is a polluted life since it makes itself. And providence has no wisdom in it. And the inevitable does not discern.

Now as for you, whatever is fitting for you to know, and those who are worthy of knowledge, will be given to them — whoever has been begotten not by the sowing of the unclean rubbing but by the First who was sent, for he is an immortal in the midst of mortal men.

[231–N]   *The perfect Savior said to him,* Before anything was revealed of those that appear, the greatness and the authority were in him, for he embraced the whole of the totalities while nothing embraced him. For he is all mind. And he is thought, and thinking, and reflecting, and rationality, and power. They all are equal powers.

They are the sources of the totalities. And their whole race from the first until the end were in his foreknowledge, that of the boundless Unbegotten Father.

[232–N]   Now a great difference exists between the imperishables and those that are perishable. *He called out, saying,* Whoever has an ear to hear about boundless things, let him hear, *and* It is those who are awake I have addressed.

[233–N]   *The perfect Savior said,* Come from the non-appearing things to the completion of those that are revealed, and she, the effluence of thought, will reveal to you how the belief in those things that are not revealed was found in those that are revealed, those that belong to the Unbegotten Father. Whoever has an ear to hear, let him hear.

[234–N]   The Lord of the Universe is not called 'Father,' but 'First Father,' the source of those that were to be revealed. Now he is the beginningless First Father who beholds himself within himself as with a mirror. He was revealed, resembling himself. And his likeness was revealed as a divine father through himself, and as Confronter over the confronted ones, the first-existing, Unbegotten Father. Indeed he is of equal age with the light that is before his countenance, but he is not equal to him in power.

[235–N]   *The perfect Savior said,* I desire that you understand that he who was revealed before the universe in the boundlessness is the self-grown, self-constructed Father who is full of shining light, and is ineffable. In the beginning he decided to have his form come to be as a great power. Immediately the beginning of that light was revealed as an immortal, androgynous man, so that through that immortal man they might attain their salvation and awake from forgetfulness through the interpreter who was sent, who is with you until the end of the poverty of the robbers. And his consort is the great Sophia, who was from the first destined in him for a yoke, through the self-begotten Father, from Immortal Man, who first was revealed in divinity and kingdom; for the Father, who is called 'Man, the Self-Father,' revealed him. He created for himself a great aeon, whose name is Ogdoad, corresponding to his greatness. He was given great authority and ruled over the creation of poverty. He created for himself gods and angels and archangels, myriads without number for retinue. This is from that light and the tri-male spirit, which is that of Sophia his consort. For from this God originated divinity and kingdom. Therefore he was called 'God of gods,' 'King of kings.'

[236–N]   First Man has his unique mind within, and thought, which is like it, reflecting, thinking, rationality, power. All the parts that exist are perfect and immortal. In respect to imperishableness, they are equal. However in respect to power, they are different, like the difference between a father and a son, and a son and a thought, and the thought and the remainder. As I said earlier, among the things that were created, the unit is first. And after everything else, that which wholly appeared was revealed by his power. And by that which was created all that was made was revealed; by that which was made was revealed that which was formed; by that which was formed, that which was named. Thus came the difference among the unbegotten ones, from beginning to end.

[237–N]   I desire that you understand that First Man is called 'Begetter, Mind who is complete in himself.' He reflected with the great Sophia, his consort, and revealed his first-begotten, androgynous son. His male name is called 'First-Begetter Son of God;' his female name is 'First-Begettress Sophia, Mother of the Universe.'

Some call her 'Love.' Now the First-begotten is called 'Christ.' Since he has authority from his Father, he created for himself a multitude of angels without number for retinue, from the spirit and the light.

[238–N]   *The perfect Savior said,* Whoever has an ear to hear, let him hear. First-Begetter Father is called 'Adam, the Eye of the Light,' because he came from the shining light with his holy angels, who are ineffable and shadowless. They rejoice continually with joy in their reflecting, which they received from their Father. This is the whole kingdom of Son of Man, the one who is called 'Son of God.' It is full of ineffable and shadowless joy, and unchanging jubilation because they rejoice over his imperishable glory, which has never been heard of until now, nor has it been revealed in the aeons that came to be after these and their worlds. I came from the Self-begotten and the First Endless Light, so that I might reveal everything to you.

[239–N]   *The Perfect Savior said,* Son of Man harmonized with Sophia, his consort, and revealed a great androgynous light. His male name is called 'Savior, Begetter of All Things.' His female name is called 'All-Begettress Sophia.' Some call her 'Pistis.' All who come into the world like a drop from the light are sent by him to the world of the Almighty, so that they might be guarded by him. And the bond of its (the drop's) forgetfulness bound it by the will of Sophia, so that the matter might be revealed through it (the bond) to the whole world of poverty concerning his (the Almighty's) arrogance and blindness, and the ignorance, because he named himself.

[240–N]   And you were sent by the son, who was sent so that you might receive light and remove yourselves from the forgetfulness of the authorities, and so that it might not again come to appearance because of you, namely, the unclean rubbing that is from the fearful fire that came from their fleshly part. Tread upon their malicious intent.

[241–N] *The perfect Savior said,* I praise you because you ask about the great aeons, because your roots are in the boundless things. And when those whom I have spoken of were revealed, the Self-Begetter Father first began to create for himself twelve aeons for retinue and twelve angels. These all are perfect and good. Through these was revealed the defect in the female.

[242–N] *The perfect Savior said,* Whoever has an ear to hear, let him hear. The first aeon is that of Son of Man, the one who is called 'First Begetter,' the one who is called 'Savior,' the one who was revealed. The second aeon is that of Man, who is called 'Adam, the Eye of the Light.' The one who embraces these is the aeon over whom there is no kingdom, the aeon of the divine, boundless eternity, the self-begotten aeon of the aeons that are in him, the aeon of the immortals, whom I have spoken of already, who is above the Seventh that was revealed by Sophia, who is the first aeon.

Now he, Immortal Man, revealed aeons and powers and kingdoms, and he gave authority to all who are revealed by him that they might exercise their desires until the last times that are above chaos. For these harmonized with each other. And he revealed every greatness, even, by the spirit, a multitude of lights which are glorious and without number, these that were designated in the beginning, that is, the first aeon, and two, and three. The first is called 'Oneness,' and 'Rest'; and each one has its own name. For they were designated 'Assembly' from the three aeons, that is, from the numerous multitude that appeared together in one. And a multitude revealed them. But because these multitudes gather together and come to a unity, we call them the 'Assembly of the Eighth.' It was revealed as androgynous, and was named partly as male and partly as female. The male is called 'Assembly,' while the female is called 'Life,' that it might be shown that from a female came the life of all the aeons. And every name was received from the time of the beginning.

For by his concurrence and his thought the powers were first revealed, who were called 'gods.' And the gods of the gods by their wisdom revealed gods. By their wisdom they revealed lords. And the lords of the lords revealed lords by their thinking. And the lords by their power revealed archangels. The archangels by their words revealed angels. By these, semblances were revealed with structure, and form, and name for all the aeons and their worlds.

And the immortals, which I have just described, all have authority from Immortal Man and Sophia, his consort, who is called 'Silence,' because in reflecting without a word all her greatness was perfected. For the imperishables, since they have the authority, each created for themselves a great kingdom in the Eighth, and also thrones, and temples, and firmaments corresponding to their greatnesses. For these all came from the will of the Mother of the Universe.

[243-N] *The perfect Savior said to them,* I desire that you understand that Sophia, the Mother of the Universe and the consort, desired by herself to bring these to existence without her male consort. But by the will of the Father of the Universe, so that his unimaginable goodness might be revealed, he created that curtain between the immortals and those that came after them, so that the consequence might follow every aeon and chaos, so that the defect of the female might live, and she (the female) might exist, although Error fights against her. And these became a curtain of a spirit. From the aeon above the effluences of light, just as I said already, a drop from the light and the spirit came down to the lower regions of the Almighty of chaos, so that he might reveal their molded forms from that drop, because it is a judgment on him, the Prime Begetter, who is called 'Yaldabaoth.' That drop revealed their molded forms through the breath for a living soul. It was withered and it slumbered in the ignorance of the soul. When it became hot from the breath of the great light of the male, and he took thought, then names were received by all who are in the world of chaos and all things that are in it, through that immortal one, when the breath blew into him. But these, when they came to be in the will of the Mother, Sophia, so that Immortal Man might piece together the garments there, were condemned as robbers, and they welcomed the blowing from that breath. But since he is psychical, he was not able to receive that power for himself until the number of chaos is complete, and when the time that is determined by the great angel is complete.

[244-N]   Whoever, then, knows the Father in pure knowledge will depart to the Father and repose in the unbegotten Father. But whoever knows him defectively will depart and repose in the rest of the Eighth. Now whoever knows the immortal spirit of light, in silence, through reflecting and desire, in truth, let him bring me signs of the invisible one, and he will become a light in the spirit of silence. Whoever knows Son of Man in knowledge and love, let him bring me a sign of Son of Man, so that he might depart to the dwellings with those who are in the Eighth.

[245-N]   Behold, I have revealed to you the name of the perfect one, the whole will of the mother of the holy angels, so that the masculine multitude may be completed here, so that there might be revealed in the aeons the boundless ones and those who came to be in the untraceable wealth of the Great Invisible Spirit, so that they all might receive from his goodness and wealth the rest that has no kingdom over it.

[246-O] But those who have not are poor, that is, those who do not possess him. And they desire him and lead astray those, who through them have become like those who possess the truth of their freedom, just as they bought us for servitude and constraint of care and fear. This person is in slavery. And he who is brought by constraint of force and threat has been guarded by God. But the entire nobility of the Fatherhood is not guarded, since he guards only him who is from him, without word and constraint, since he is united with his will, he who belongs only to the Ennoia of the Fatherhood, to make it perfect and ineffable through the living water, to be with you mutually in wisdom, not only in word of hearing but in deed and fulfilled word. For the perfect ones are worthy to be established in this way and to be united with me, in order that they may not share in any enmity, in a good friendship. I accomplish everything through the Good One, for this is the union of the truth, that they should have no adversary. But everyone who brings division — and he will learn no wisdom at all because he brings division and is not a friend — is hostile to them all. But he who lives in harmony and friendship of brotherly love, naturally and not artificially, completely and not partially, this person is truly the desire of the Father. He is the universal one and perfect love.

[247-Q] And you therefore celebrate the remembrance of my death, i.e. the passover; then will one of you who stands beside me be thrown into prison for my name's sake, and he will be very grieved and sorrowful, for while you celebrate the passover he who is in custody did not celebrate it with you. And I will send my power in the form of my angel, and the door of the prison will open, and he will come out and come to you to watch with you and to rest. And when you complete my Agape and my remembrance at the crowing of the cock, he will again be taken and thrown in prison for a testimony, until he comes out to preach, as I have commanded you.

And we said to him, 'O Lord, have you then not completed the drinking of the passover? Must we, then, do it again?'

And he said to us, Yes, until I come from the Father with my wounds.

[248-Q]   Truly I say to you, you will be my brothers and companions, for my Father has delighted in you and in those who will believe in me through you. Truly I say to you, such and so great a joy has my Father prepared for you that angels and powers desired and will desire to view and to see it, but they will not be allowed to see the greatness of my Father.

[249-Q]   Truly I say to you, as the Father awakened me from the dead, in the same manner you also will arise in the flesh, and he will cause you to rise up above the heavens to the place of which I have spoken to you from the beginning, which he who sent me has prepared for you.

[250-Q]   Truly I say to you, the flesh of every man will rise with his soul alive and his spirit.

[251-Q]   I know that in faith and with your whole heart you question me. Therefore I am glad because of you. Truly I say to you I am pleased, and my Father in me rejoices, that you thus inquire and ask. Your boldness makes me rejoice, and it affords yourselves life.

[252-Q]   But to you I have given that you should be children of the light in God and should be pure from all wickedness and from all power of the judgment; and to those who believe in me through you I will do the same, and as I have said and promised to you, that he should go out of prison and should be rescued from the chains and the spears and the terrible fire.

[253-Q]   *And he said to us,* Truly I say to you, you and all who believe and also they who yet will believe in him who sent me I will cause to rise up into heaven, to the place which the Father has prepared for the elect and most elect, the Father who will give the rest that he has promised, and eternal life.

[254-Q]   But much more blessed will they be who do not see me and yet believe in me, for they will be called children of the kingdom and will be perfect in the perfect one; to these I will become eternal life in the kingdom of my Father.

[255-Q]   As my Father has done through me, I will also do through you in that I am with you, and I will give you my peace and my spirit and my power, that it may happen to you that they believe. Also to them will this power be given and transmitted that they may give it to the Gentiles.

[256-Q]   Do not be grieved. Truly I say to you, you are my brothers, companions in the kingdom of heaven with my Father, for so has it pleased him. Truly I say to you, also to those whom you shall have taught and who have become believers in me will I give this hope.

[257-Q]   *And we said to him again, 'O Lord, will the Gentiles then not say, 'Where is their God?' He answered and said to us,* Thus will the elect be revealed, in that they go out after they have been afflicted by such a distress.

[258-Q]   Whoever has done the glorification of my Father, he is the dwelling-place of my Father.

[259-Q]   But those who desire to see the face of God and who do not regard the person of the sinful rich and who do not fear the men who lead them astray, but reprove them, they will be crowned in the presence of the Father, as also those who reprove their neighbors will be saved. This is a son of wisdom and of faith. But if he does not become a son of wisdom, then he will hate and persecute and not turn towards his brother, and will despise him and cast him away. But those who walk in truth and in the knowledge of faith in me and have the knowledge of wisdom and perseverance for righteousness' sake, in that men despise those who strive for poverty and they nevertheless endure — great is their reward. Those who are reviled, tormented, persecuted, since they are destitute and men are arrogant against them and they hunger and thirst and because they have persevered — blessed will they be in heaven, and they will be there with me always. Woe to those who hate and despise them! And their end is for destruction.

[260-Q]   *And he said to us,* Adam was given the power that he might choose what he wanted from the two; and he chose the light and stretched out his hand and took it and left the darkness and withdrew from it. Likewise every man is given the ability to believe in the light; this is the life of the Father who sent me.

[261-Q]   And whoever does my commandment and keeps it will be a son of the light, i.e. of my Father. And for those who keep and do it, for their sake I came down from heaven; I, the word, became flesh and died, teaching and guiding, that some shall be saved, but the others eternally ruined, being punished by fire in flesh and spirit. *And we said to him, 'O Lord, we are truly troubled on their account.' And he said to us,* You do well, for so are the righteous anxious about the sinners, and they pray and implore God and ask him. *And we said to him, 'O Lord, does no one entreat you?' And he said to us,* Yes, I will hear the requests of the righteous concerning them.

[262-Q]   Are all fathers and all servants, all teachers? *And we said to him, 'O Lord, did you not say, "Do not call anyone on earth father and master, for one is your father and teacher, he who is in heaven?"' Now you say to us that we should like you become fathers to many children and also teachers and servants. And he answered and said to us,* You have rightly said. Truly I say to you, all who have listened to you and have believed in me will receive the light of the seal that is in my hand, and through me you will become fathers and teachers.

[263-Q]   *And we said to him, 'O Lord, how is it possible for these three to be in one?' And he answered and said to us,* Truly, truly I say to you, you will be called fathers, for you, full of love and compassion, have revealed to them what is in heaven for by my hand they will receive the baptism of life and forgiveness of sin. And teachers, for you have delivered to them my word without anguish and have warned them and they have turned back in the things for which you rebuked them. And you were not afraid of their riches and did not respect the person, but you kept the commandment of the Father and did it. And you have a reward with my heavenly Father; and they shall have forgiveness of sins and eternal life and a share of the kingdom.

[264-Q]   If you have seen with your eyes how someone sins, then correct him, you alone. If he listens to you, then you have won him. But if he does not listen to you, then come out with one or at most two others; correct your brother. But if he even then does not listen to you, so shall he be to you as a Gentile and a tax collector.

If you hear something, then do not give any belief against your brother and do not slander and do not love to listen to slander. For it is written, 'Let your ear listen to nothing against your brother, but only if you have seen, censure, correct, and convert him.' *And we said to him, 'Lord, you have taught and exhorted us in everything. But, Lord, among the believers who among them believe in the preaching of*

*your name should there be dissension and dispute and envy and confusion
and hatred and distress? For you have nevertheless said, 'They will find
fault with one another and have not regarded the person.' Do these sin who
hate the one who has corrected them? And he answered and said to us,*
Now why will the judgment take place? That the wheat may be put
in its barn and its chaff thrown into the fire.

[265-Q]   Do not fear what will happen not with many, but only
with few.

[266-R]   *. . . and I heard him also saying to my Lord, 'Jesus, the men you
have chosen still disbelieve you.' And my Lord said to him,* You are right;
for they are men.

[267-R]   *And my Lord stood in the middle of the cave and gave light to it
and said,* John, for the people below in Jerusalem I am being crucified and pierced with lances and reeds and given vinegar and gall to
drink. But to you I am speaking, and listen to what I speak. I put
into your mind to come up to this mountain so that you may hear
what a disciple should learn from his teacher and a man from God.

[268-R]   John, there must be one man to hear these things from
me; for I need one who is ready to hear. This Cross of Light is
sometimes called Logos by me for your sakes, sometimes mind,
sometimes Jesus, sometimes Christ, sometimes a door, sometimes a
way, sometimes bread, sometimes seed, sometimes resurrection,
sometimes Son, sometimes Father, sometimes Spirit, sometimes
life, sometimes truth, sometimes faith, sometimes grace; and so it is
called for men's sake.

But what it truly is, as known in itself and spoken to us, is this: it
is the distinction of all things, and the strong uplifting of what is
firmly fixed out of what is unstable, and the harmony of wisdom,

being wisdom in harmony. But there are places on the right and on the left, powers, authorities, principalities and demons, activities, threatenings, passions, devils, Satan and the inferior root from which the nature of transient things proceeded.

[269-R]   This cross then is that which has united all things by the word and which has separated off what is transitory and inferior, which has also compacted all things into one. But this is not that wooden Cross which you shall see when you go down from here; nor am I the man who is on the Cross, I whom now you do not see but only hear my voice. I was taken to be what I am not, I who am not what for many others I was; but what they will say of me is mean and unworthy of me. Since then the place of my rest is neither to be seen nor told, much more shall I, the Lord of this place, be neither seen nor told.

[270-R]   The multitude around the cross that is not of one form is the inferior nature. And those whom you saw in the Cross, even if they have not yet one form — not every member of him who has come down has yet been gathered together. But when human nature is taken up, and the race that comes to me and obeys my voice, then he who now hears me shall be united with this race and shall no longer be what he now is, but shall be above them as I am now. For so long as you do not call yourself mine, I am not what I am; but if you hear me, you also as hearer shall be as I am, and I shall be what I was, when you are as I am with myself; for from me you are what I am. Therefore ignore the many and despise those who are outside the mystery; for you must know that I am wholly with the Father, and the Father with me.

[271-R]   So then I have suffered none of those things which they will say of me; even that suffering which I showed to you and to the rest in my dance, I will that it be called a mystery.

[272-S]   Ask then, and I will tell you all you wish to know. And I myself will make known to you what you do not say.

[273-S]   Blessed are you, Bartholomew my beloved, because you saw these mysteries. This was one of the avenging angels who stand before my Father's throne. He sent this angel to me. And for this reason he would not go up, because he wished to destroy the power of the world. But when I commanded him to go up, a flame issued from his hand, and after he had rent the veil of the temple, he divided it into two parts as a testimony to the children of Israel for my passion, because they crucified me.

[274-S]   *And when he had said this, he said to the apostles*: Wait for me in this place; for today a sacrifice is offered in paradise, that I may receive it after my arrival.
    And Bartholomew said to him: 'Lord, what sacrifice is offered in Paradise?'
    Jesus answered: The souls of the righteous, when they leave the body, go to paradise, and unless I am present there they cannot enter.
    Bartholomew asked: 'Lord, how many souls leave the world every day?'
    Jesus answered: Thirty thousand.
    And again Bartholomew asked: 'Lord, when you lived among us, did you receive the sacrifices in paradise?'
    Jesus answered: Verily, I say to you, my beloved, even when I taught among you, I sat at the right hand of the Father and received the sacrifices in paradise.
    And Bartholomew said: 'Lord, if thirty thousand souls leave this world daily, how many are admitted into paradise?'
    Jesus answered: Only three.
    Bartholomew again asked: 'Lord how many souls are born into the world every day?'

Jesus answered: Only one over and above those who leave the world.

[275-S] The head of the man is Christ, but the head of the woman is the man.

[276-S] Ask me what you wish, so that I can teach you and show you. For there are still seven days, and then I ascend to my Father and shall no more appear to you in this form.

But they, hesitating, said to him: 'Lord, show us the abyss, as you promised us.'

He answered: It is not good for you to see the abyss. But if you wish it, I will keep my promise. Come, follow me and see. *And he led them to a place called Cherubim, that is, place of truth. And he beckoned to the angels of the west. And the earth was rolled up like a papyrus roll, and the abyss was exposed to their eyes. When the apostles saw it, they fell on their faces. But Jesus said to them*: Did I not say to you that it was not good for you to see the abyss? *And he again beckoned to the angels, and the abyss was covered up.*

[277-S] *And Bartholomew was afraid, and said: 'Lord Jesus, give me a hem of your garment, that I may venture to approach him.'*

Jesus answered him: You cannot have a hem of my garment, for it is not the garment which I wore before I was crucified.

[278-S] Were not all things made by my word and according to the plan of my Father? The spirits were made subject to Solomon himself. Go therefore, since you have been commanded to do so in my name, and ask him what you wish.

[279-S] *And again Bartholomew said to him, 'Lord, may I reveal these mysteries to every man?'*

Jesus answered him: Bartholomew, my beloved, entrust them to all who are faithful and can keep them for themselves. For there are some who are worthy of them; but there are also others to whom they ought not to be entrusted, for they are boasters, drunkards, proud, merciless, idolaters, seducers to fornication, slanderers, teachers of falsehood, and doers of all the works of the devil, and therefore they are not worthy that they should be entrusted to them. These things are also to be kept secret because of those who cannot contain them. For all who can contain them shall have a share in them. As regards this, therefore, my beloved, I have spoken to you, for you are blessed and all who are akin to you in having this message entrusted to them, for all who contain it shall receive all they wish in all times of my judgment.

[280-U]   Hast thou seen the companies of the fathers? As is their rest, so also is the honor and glory of those who will be persecuted for my righteousness' sake.

[281-V]   Eat every plant, but that which has bitterness eat not.

[282-V]   *For the Lord says*: You will be as sheep in the midst of wolves.
   But Peter answered him and said: 'What if the wolves tear the sheep to pieces?'
   Jesus said to Peter: Let the sheep not fear the wolves after death; you also fear not them who kill you, but otherwise cannot do anything to you; but fear him who after your death has power over body and soul to cast them into hell-fire.

[283-V]   My brethren are those who do the will of my Father.

[284-W]   Wherefore ye do err, because ye do not know the true things of the Scriptures, and on this account also ye know nothing of the power of God.

[285–W]   Be ye good money changers.

[286–W]   Wherefore do ye not understand what is reasonable in the Scriptures?

[287–X]   The unmarried think day and night on godly things.

[288–X]   Oh! as a virgin, as a woman, so is the mystery of resurrection which you have shown to me, you who in the beginning of the world did institute vain feasts for yourselves and delighted in the wantonness of the Gentiles and behaved in the same way as those who take delight therein.

[289–X]   He that believes on me will also do the works that I do, and will do greater works than these.

[290–X]   I will give them, *he says*, the eternal morning star, as I myself received it from my Father.

[291–X]   I will confess them . . . before my Father and his angels in heaven.

[292–X]   . . . *the Lord says*: To him that overcometh will I grant to sit at my right hand in my throne, even as I have overcome and sit on the right hand of my Father in his throne to all ages for ever and ever. Amen.

VI

Hymns and Prayers

[1–A]   In this manner, therefore, pray:
Our Father in heaven,
Hallowed be Your name.
Your kingdom come.
Your will be done
On earth as it is in heaven.
Give us this day our daily bread.
And forgive us our debts,
As we forgive our debtors.
And do not lead us into temptation,
But deliver us from the evil one.
For Yours is the kingdom and the power
and the glory forever. Amen.

[2–A]   I thank You, Father, Lord of heaven and earth, that You
have hidden these things from the wise and prudent and have re-

vealed them to babes. Even so, Father, for so it seemed good in Your sight. All things have been delivered to Me by My Father, and no one knows the Son except the Father. Nor does anyone know the Father except the Son, and the one to whom the Son wills to reveal Him.

[3–A]   O My Father, if it is possible, let this cup pass from Me; nevertheless, not as I will, but as You will.

[4–A]   O My Father, if this cup cannot pass away from Me unless I drink it, Your will be done.

[5–B]   Abba, Father, all things are possible to thee; remove this cup from me: yet not what I will, but what thou wilt.

[6–C]   *In that hour Jesus rejoiced in the Spirit and said,* I thank You, Father, Lord of heaven and earth, that You have hidden these things from the wise and prudent and revealed them to babes. Even so, Father, for so it seemed good in Your sight.

[7–C]   *So He said to them,* When you pray, say;
   Our Father in heaven,
   Hallowed be Your name.
   Your kingdom come.
   Your will be done
   On earth as it is in heaven.
   Give us day by day our daily bread.
   And forgive us our sins,
   For we also forgive everyone who is indebted to us.
   And do not lead us into temptation,
   But deliver us from the evil one.

[8–D]   *And Jesus lifted up his eyes and said,* Father, I thank thee that thou hast heard me. I knew that thou hearest me always, but I have said this on account of the people standing by, that they may believe that thou didst send me.

[9–D]   *When Jesus had spoken these words, he lifted up his eyes to heaven and said,* Father, the hour has come; glorify thy Son that the Son may glorify thee, since thou hast given him power over all flesh, to give eternal life to all whom thou hast given him. And this is eternal life, that they know thee the only true God, and Jesus Christ whom thou hast sent. I glorified thee on earth, having accomplished the work which thou gavest me to do; and now, Father, glorify thou me in thy own presence with the glory which I had with thee before the world was made. I have manifested thy name to the men whom thou gavest me out of the world; thine they were, and thou gavest them to me, and they have kept thy word.

Now they know that everything that thou hast given me is from thee; for I have given them the words which thou gavest me, and they have received them and know in truth that I came from thee; and they have believed that thou didst send me. I am praying for them; I am not praying for the world but for those whom thou hast given me, for they are thine; all mine are thine, and thine are mine, and I am glorified in them. And now I am no more in the world, but they are in the world, and I am coming to thee. Holy Father, keep them in thy name, which thou hast given me, that they may be one, even as we are one.

While I was with them, I kept them in thy name, which thou hast given me; I have guarded them, and none of them is lost but the son of perdition, that the scripture might be fulfilled. But now I am coming to thee; and these things I speak in the world, that they may have my joy fulfilled in themselves. I have given them thy word; and the world has hated them because they are not of the world, even as

I am not of the world. I do not pray that thou shouldst take them out of the world, but that thou shouldst keep them from the evil one. They are not of the world, even as I am not of the world. Sanctify them in the truth; thy word is truth. As thou didst send me into the world, so I have sent them into the world. And for their sake I consecrate myself, that they also may be consecrated in truth.

I do not pray for these only, but also for those who believe in me through their word, that they may all be one; even as thou, Father, art in me, and I in thee, that they also may be in us, so that the world may believe that thou hast sent me. The glory which thou hast given me I have given to them, that they may be one even as we are one, I in them and thou in me, that they may become perfectly one, so that the world may know that thou hast sent me and hast loved them even as thou hast loved me. Father, I desire that they also, whom thou hast given me, may be with me where I am, to behold my glory which thou hast given me in thy love for me before the foundation of the world. O righteous Father, the world has not known thee, but I have known thee; and these know that thou hast sent me. I made known to them thy name, and I will make it known, that the love with which thou hast loved me may be in them, and I in them.

[10–M]   Hear us, Father, just as thou hast heard thine only-begotten Son and hast taken him to thyself and given him rest from many labors. Thou art he whose power is great, and thy weapons are *(. . .) light (. . .) living (. . . who) cannot be touched (. . .) the word of (. . .) repentance of life (. . . from) thee. Thou art the remembrance and all the serenity of the solitary ones. Again hear us, just as thou hast heard thine elect ones. These by thy sacrifice enter in with their good deeds, they who have redeemed their souls from these blind limbs in order that they might exist forever. Amen.

---

*(. . .) Indicates a gap in the original text.

[11-R]   *Then bidding us make as it were a ring, by holding each others'*
hands, with Him in the midst, He said:

Answer 'Amen' to Me.

Then He began to hymn a hymn and say:

Glory to Thee, Father!

(*And we going round in a ring answered to Him:*)

Amen!

Glory to Thee, Word [Logos]!

Amen!

Glory to thee, Grace [Charis]!

Amen!

Glory to Thee, Spirit!

Glory to Thee, Holy One!

Glory to thy Glory!

Amen!

We praise Thee, O Father;

We give Thanks to Thee, O Light;

In whom Darkness dwells not!

Amen!

[For what we give thanks to the Logos.] [Or, For what we give
thanks, I say:]

I would be saved; and I would save.

Amen!

I would be loosed; and I would loose.

Amen!

I would be wounded; and I would wound. [Or, I would be
pierced; and I would pierce. Another reading has: I would be dissolved (or consumed for love); and I would dissolve.]

Amen!

I would be begotten; and I would beget.

Amen!

I would eat; and I would be eaten

Amen!

[I would understand; and] I would be understood; being all Understanding [Nous].

I would be washed; and I would wash.

Amen!

(Grace leadeth the dance.)

I would pipe; dance ye all.

Amen!

I would play a dirge; lament ye all.

Amen!

The one Ogdoad sounds [or plays] with us.

Amen!

The Twelfth Number above leadeth the dance.

Amen!

All whose nature is to dance [doth dance].

Amen!

Who danceth not, knows not what is being done.

Amen!

I would flee; and I would stay.

Amen!

I would be adorned; and I would adorn.

Amen!

I would be atoned; and I would atone.

Amen!

I have no dwelling; and I have dwellings.

Amen!

I have no place; and I have places.

Amen!

I have no temple; and I have temples.

Amen!

I am a lamp to thee who seest Me.

Amen!

I am a mirror to thee who understandest Me.
Amen!
I am a door to thee who knockest at Me.
Amen!
I am a way to thee a wayfarer.
Amen!
Now answer to My dancing!
See thyself in Me who speak;
And seeing what I do,
Keep silence on My Mysteries.
Understand, by dancing, what I do;
For thine is the Passion of Man
That I am to suffer.
Thou couldst not at all be conscious
Of what thou dost suffer,
Were I not sent as thy Word by the Father.
Seeing what I suffer,
Thou sawest Me as suffering;
And seeing, thou didst not stand,
But wast moved wholly,
Moved to be wise.
Thou hast Me for a couch; rest thou upon Me.
Who I am thou shalt know when I depart.
What now I am seen to be, that I am not.
[But what I am] thou shalt see when thou comest.
If thou hadst known how to suffer.
Thou wouldst have power not to suffer.
Know then how to suffer, and thou hast power not to suffer.
That which thou knowest not, I Myself will teach thee
I am thy God, not the Betrayer's.
I would be kept in time with holy souls.
In Me know thou the Word of Wisdom.

Say thou to me again:
Glory to Thee, Father!
Glory to Thee, Word!
Glory to Thee, Holy Spirit!
But as for Me, if thou wouldst know what I was:
In a word I am the Word who did play [or dance] all things, and was not shamed at all.
'Twas I who leaped [and danced].
But do thou understand all, and, understanding, say:
Glory to Thee, Father!
Amen!

(And having danced these things with us, Beloved, the Lord went forth. And we, as though beside ourselves, or wakened out of deep sleep, fled each our several ways.)

[12–S]   I am good to you. Alleluia. I am meek and kind to you. Alleluia. Glory be to thee, O Lord. For I give myself to all who desire me. Alleluia. Glory be to Thee, O Lord, world without end. Amen. Alleluia.

VII

Jesus Laughing

[1-H]   *And as soon as Christ went down into the water he came out laughing at everything of this world, not because he considers it a trifle, but because he is full of contempt for it. He who wants to enter the Kingdom of heaven will attain it.*

[2-J]   *The Savior said to me,* He whom you saw on the tree, glad and laughing, this is the living Jesus.

[3-J]   *And I saw someone about to approach us resembling him, even him who was laughing on the tree.*

[4-J]   But he who stands near him is the living Savior, the first in him, whom they seized and released, who stands joyfully looking at those who did him violence, while they are divided among themselves. Therefore he laughs at their lack of perception, knowing that they are born blind.

[5-N]   *The Savior laughed and said to them,* What are you thinking about? Why are you perplexed?

[6-O]   But I [Jesus] laughed joyfully when I examined his empty glory.

[7-O]   And I was laughing at their ignorance.

[8-P]   *And he smiled and said,* Do not think it is, as Moses said, 'above the waters.' No, but when she had seen the wickedness which had happened, and the theft which her son had committed, she repented.

[9-P]   *The savior smiled and said,* The serpent taught them to eat from wickedness, begetting, lust, and the destruction, that he might be useful to him.

[10-P]   *And I said, 'Lord, where will the souls of these go when they have come out of their flesh?' And he smiled and said to me,* The soul in which the power will become superior to the despicable spirit, she is strong and she flees from evil . . .

_____

Note: See *Afterword: Jesus Laughing*

VIII

Diverse Doctrine

[1–A] *But He answered and said,* It is written, 'Man shall not live by bread alone, but by every word that proceeds from the mouth of God.'

[2–A] *Then He said to them,* Follow Me, and I will make you fishers of men.

[3–A] You are the salt of the earth; but if the salt loses its flavor, how shall it be seasoned? It is then good for nothing but to be thrown out and trampled underfoot by men.

[4–A] If your right eye causes you to sin, pluck it out and cast it from you; for it is more profitable for you that one of your members perish, than for your whole body to be cast into hell. And if your right hand causes you to sin, cut it off and cast it from you; for it is more profitable for you that one of your members perish, than for your whole body to be cast into hell. Furthermore it has been said,

'Whoever divorces his wife, let him give her a certificate of divorce.'
But I say to you that whoever divorces his wife for any reason except
sexual immorality causes her to commit adultery; and whoever marries a woman who is divorced commits adultery.

[5–A]   Moreover, when you fast, do not be like the hypocrites, with
a sad countenance. For they disfigure their faces that they may appear to men to be fasting. Assuredly, I say to you, they have their reward. But you, when you fast, anoint your head and wash your face,
so that you do not appear to men to be fasting, but to your Father
who is in the secret place; and your Father who sees in secret will
reward you openly.

[6–A]   No one can serve two masters; for either he will hate the
one and love the other; or else he will be loyal to the one and despise the other. You cannot serve God and mammon.

[7–A]   And why do you look at the speck in your brother's eye, but
do not consider the plank in your own eye? Or how can you say to
your brother, 'Let me remove the speck from your eye'; and look, a
plank is in your own eye? Hypocrite! First remove the plank from
your own eye, and then you will see clearly to remove the speck
from your brother's eye.

[8–A]   Even so, every good tree bears good fruit, but a bad tree bears
bad fruit. A good tree cannot bear bad fruit, nor can a bad tree bear
good fruit. Every tree that does not bear good fruit is cut down and
thrown into the fire. Therefore by their fruits you will know them.

[9–A]   Therefore whoever hears these sayings of Mine, and does
them, I will liken him to a wise man who built his house on the rock:
and the rain descended, the floods came, and the winds blew and

beat on that house; and it did not fall, for it was founded on the rock. But everyone who hears these sayings of Mine, and does not do them, will be like a foolish man who built his house on the sand: and the rain descended, the floods came, and the winds blew and beat on that house; and it fell. And great was its fall.

[10–A] *Then Jesus put out His hand and touched him, saying,* I am willing; be cleansed. *Immediately his leprosy was cleansed. And Jesus said to him,* See that you tell no one; but go your way, show yourself to the priest, and offer the gift that Moses commanded, as a testimony to them.

[11–A] *And Jesus said to him,* I will come and heal him.

[12–A] *When Jesus heard it, He marveled, and said to those who followed,* Assuredly, I say to you, I have not found such great faith, not even in Israel! And I say to you that many will come from east and west, and sit down with Abraham, Isaac, and Jacob, in the kingdom of heaven. But the sons of the kingdom will be cast out into outer darkness. There will be weeping and gnashing of teeth. *Then Jesus said to the centurion,* Go your way; and as you have believed, let it be done for you. *And his servant was healed that same hour.*

[13–A] *But He said to them,* Why are you fearful, O you of little faith? *Then He arose and rebuked the winds and the sea, and there was a great calm.*

[14–A] *Then behold, they brought to Him a paralytic lying on a bed. When Jesus saw their faith, He said to the paralytic,* Son, be of good cheer; your sins are forgiven you. *And at once some of the scribes said within themselves, 'This Man blasphemes!' But Jesus, knowing their thoughts, said,* Why do you think evil in your hearts? For which is easier, to say, 'Your sins are forgiven you,' or to say, 'Arise and walk'? But that you may know that the Son of Man has power on earth to forgive sins — *then He said to the paralytic*, Arise, take up your bed, and go to your house.

[15-A]   No one puts a piece of unshrunk cloth on an old garment; for the patch pulls away from the garment, and the tear is made worse. Nor do they put new wine into old wineskins, or else the wineskins break, the wine is spilled, and the wineskins are ruined. But they put new wine into new wineskins, and both are preserved.

[16-A]   *But Jesus turned around, and when He saw her He said*, Be of good cheer, daughter; your faith has made you well. *And the woman was made well from that hour.*

[17-A]   *And when He had come into the house, the blind men came to Him. And Jesus said to them*, Do you believe that I am able to do this? *They said to Him, 'Yes, Lord.' Then He touched their eyes, saying*, According to your faith let it be to you. *And their eyes were opened. And Jesus sternly warned them, saying*, See that no one knows it.

[18-A]   Heal the sick, cleanse the lepers, raise the dead, cast out demons. Freely you have received, freely give. Provide neither gold nor silver nor copper in your money belts, nor bag for your journey, nor two tunics, nor sandals, nor staffs; for a worker is worthy of his food. Now whatever city or town you enter, inquire who in it is worthy, and stay there till you go out. And when you go into a household, greet it. If the household is worthy, let your peace come upon it. But if it is not worthy, let your peace return to you.

[19-A]   And you will be hated by all for My name's sake. But he who endures to the end will be saved. When they persecute you in this city, flee to another. For assuredly, I say to you, you will not have gone through the cities of Israel before the Son of Man comes.

[20-A]   *Jesus answered and said to them,* Go and tell John the things which you hear and see: The blind see and the lame walk; the lepers are cleansed and the deaf hear; the dead are raised up and the poor have the gospel preached to them. And blessed is he who is not offended because of Me.

[21-A]   *As they departed, Jesus began to say to the multitudes concerning John:* What did you go out into the wilderness to see? A reed shaken by the wind? But what did you go out to see? A man clothed in soft garments? Indeed, those who wear soft clothing are in kings' houses. But what did you go out to see? A prophet? Yes, I say to you, and more than a prophet. For this is he of whom it is written: 'Behold, I send my messenger before Your face, who will prepare Your way before You.'

[22-A]   For John came neither eating nor drinking, and they say, 'He has a demon.' The Son of Man came eating and drinking, and they say, 'Look, a glutton and a winebibber, a friend of tax collectors and sinners!' But wisdom is justified by her children.

[23-A]   *But he said to them,* Have you not read what David did when he was hungry, he and those who were with him: how he entered the house of God and ate the showbread which was not lawful for him to eat, nor for those who were with him, but only for the priests? Or have you not read in the law that on the Sabbath the priests in the temple profane the Sabbath, and are blameless?

[24-A]   *But Jesus knew their thoughts, and said to them:* Every kingdom divided against itself is brought to desolation, and every city or house divided against itself will not stand. If Satan casts out Satan, he is divided against himself. How then will his kingdom stand? And if I cast out demons by Beelzebub, by whom do your sons cast them out? Therefore they shall be your judges. But if I cast out demons by the Spirit of God, surely the kingdom of God has come upon you. Or how can one enter a strong man's house and plunder his goods, unless he first binds the strong man? And then he will plunder his house.

[25-A]   But I say to you that for every idle word men may speak, they will give account of it in the day of judgment. For by your words you will be justified, and by your words you will be condemned.

[26-A]   Therefore I speak to them in parables, because seeing they do not see, and hearing they do not hear, nor do they understand.

[27-A]   *But Jesus said to them,* They do not need to go away. You give them something to eat.

[28-A]   *But immediately Jesus spoke to them, saying,* Be of good cheer! It is I; do not be afraid.

[29-A]   *And immediately Jesus stretched out His hand and caught him, and said to him,* O you of little faith, why did you doubt?

[30-A]   *But He answered and said,* It is not good to take the children's bread and throw it to the little dogs.

[31-A]   *Then Jesus answered and said to her,* O woman, great is your faith! Let it be to you as you desire. *And her daughter was healed from that very hour.*

[32–A]   *Now Jesus called his disciples to Himself and said,* I have compassion on the multitude, because they have now continued with Me three days and have nothing to eat. And I do not want to send them away hungry, lest they faint on the way.

[33–A]   O you of little faith, why do you reason among yourselves because you have brought no bread? Do you not yet understand, or remember the five loaves of the five thousand and how many baskets you took up? Nor the seven loaves of the four thousand and how many large baskets you took up? How is it you do not understand that I did not speak to you concerning bread? — but to beware of the leaven of the Pharisees and Sadducees.

[34–A]   *When Jesus came into the region of Caesarea Philippi, He asked His disciples, saying,* Who do men say that I, the Son of Man, am?
  So they said, 'Some say John the Baptist, some Elijah, and others Jeremiah or one of the prophets.'
  He said to them, But who do you say that I am? *Simon Peter answered and said, 'You are the Christ, the Son of the living God.'*
  Jesus answered and said to him, Blessed are you, Simon Bar-Jonah, for flesh and blood has not revealed this to you, but My Father who is in heaven. And I also say to you that you are Peter, and on this rock I will build My church, and the gates of Hades shall not prevail against it. And I will give you the keys of the kingdom of heaven, and whatever you bind on earth will be bound in heaven, and whatever you loose on earth will be loosed in heaven.

[35–A]   For the Son of Man will come in the glory of His Father with His angels, and then He will reward each according to his works. Assuredly, I say to you, there are some standing here who shall not taste death till they see the Son of Man coming in His kingdom.

[36–A] *But Jesus came and touched them and said*, Arise, and do not be afraid.

[37–A] *Now as they came down from the mountain, Jesus commanded them, saying*, Tell the vision to no one until the Son of Man is risen from the dead.

And His disciples asked Him, saying, 'Why then do the scribes say that Elijah must come first?'

Jesus answered and said to them, Indeed, Elijah is coming first and will restore all things. But I say to you that Elijah has come already, and they did not know him but did to him whatever they wished. Likewise the Son of Man is also about to suffer at their hands.

[38–A] *Then Jesus answered and said*, O faithless and perverse generation, how long shall I be with you? How long shall I bear with you? Bring him here to Me.

[39–A] What do you think, Simon? From whom do the kings of the earth take customs or taxes, from their sons or from strangers?

Peter said to Him, 'From strangers.'

Jesus said to him, Then the sons are free. Nevertheless, lest we offend them, go to the sea, cast in a hook, and take the fish that comes up first. And when you have opened its mouth, you will find a piece of money; take that and give it to them for Me and you.

[40–A] Again I say to you that if two of you agree on earth concerning anything that they ask, it will be done for them by My Father in heaven. For where two or three are gathered together in My name, I am there in the midst of them.

[41–A] *But He said to them*, All cannot accept this saying, but only those to whom it has been given: for there are eunuchs who were born thus from their mother's womb, and there are eunuchs who were made eunuchs by men, and there are eunuchs who have made themselves eunuchs for the kingdom of heaven's sake. He who is able to accept it, let him accept it.

[42–A]   *But Jesus looked at them and said to them*, With men this is impossible, but with God all things are possible.

[43–A]   *But Jesus answered and said*, You do not know what you ask. Are you able to drink the cup that I am about to drink, and be baptized with the baptism that I am baptized with?
   They said to Him, 'We are able.'
   So He said to them, You will indeed drink My cup, and be baptized with the baptism that I am baptized with; but to sit on My right hand and on My left is not Mine to give, but it is for those for whom it is prepared by My Father.

[44–A]   Go into the village over against you, and straightway ye shall find an ass tied, and a colt with her: loose them and bring them unto Me. And if any man say ought unto to you, ye shall say, 'The Lord hath need of them;' and straightway he will send them.

[45–A]   *And He said unto them*, It is written, 'My house shall be called the house of prayer; but ye have made it a den of thieves.'

[46–A]   *And Jesus saith unto them*, Yea; have ye never read, 'Out of the mouths of babes and sucklings thou hast perfected praise'?

[47–A]   *And Jesus answered and said unto them*, I also will ask you one thing, which if ye tell Me, I in like wise will tell you by what authority I do these things. The baptism of John whence was it? From heaven, or of men?

And they reasoned with themselves, saying, 'If we shall say, "From heaven"; He will say unto us, "Why did ye not then believe him?" But if we shall say, "Of men"; we fear the people; for all hold John as a prophet.' And they answered Jesus, and said, 'We cannot tell.'

And He said unto them, Neither tell I you by what authority I do these things.

[48–A]   *While the Pharisees were gathered together, Jesus asked them, saying,* 'What think ye of Christ? Whose son is He?'

They say unto Him, 'The son of David.'

He saith unto them, How then doth David in spirit call Him 'Lord,' saying, 'The Lord said unto my Lord, "Sit thou on my right hand, till I make thine enemies thy footstool."' If David then call Him 'Lord,' how is He his son?

[49–A]   *And as they did eat, he said,* Verily I say unto you, that one of you shall betray me.

[50–A]   The Son of Man goeth as it is written of Him; but woe unto that man by whom the Son of Man is betrayed! It had been good for that man if he had not been born.

[51–A]   *Then he saith unto them,* My soul is exceeding sorrowful, even unto death: tarry ye here, and watch with me.

[52–A]   *Then cometh he to his disciples, and saith unto them,* Sleep on now, and take your rest: behold, the hour is at hand, and the Son of Man is betrayed in the hands of sinners. Rise, let us be going: behold, he is at hand that doth betray me.

[53–A]   *And about the ninth hour Jesus cried with a loud voice, saying,* E'-li, E'-li, la'-ma sa-bach'-tha-ni? *that is to say,* My God, my God, why hast thou forsaken me?

[54–B] *When Jesus heard it, he said to them,* Those who are well have no need of a physician, but those who are sick. I came not to call the righteous, but sinners, to repentance.

[55–B] *And he awoke and rebuked the wind, and said to the sea,* Peace! Be still! *And the wind ceased, and there was a great calm. He said to them,* Why are you afraid? Have you no faith?

[56–B] Do not fear, only believe.

[57–B] For what can a man give in return for his life?

[58–B] *And Jesus said to him,* If you can! All things are possible to him who believes.

[59–B] . . . *for he was teaching his disciples, saying to them,* The Son of man will be delivered into the hands of men, and they will kill him; and when he is killed, after three days he will rise.

[60–B] *And he sat down and called the twelve; and he said to them,* If any one would be first, he must be last of all and servant of all.

[61–B] *But Jesus said to them,* For your hardness of heart he wrote you this commandment. But from the beginning of creation, 'God made them male and female.' 'For this reason a man shall leave his father and mother and be joined to his wife, and the two shall become one flesh.' So they are no longer two but one flesh. What therefore God has joined together, let not man put asunder.

[62–B] *And he said to them,* Whoever divorces his wife and marries another, commits adultery against her; and if she divorces her husband and marries another, she commits adultery.

[63–B] *And Jesus said to him,* Go your way; your faith has made you well. *And immediately he received his sight and followed him on the way.*

[64–B] *Jesus said to them,* Render to Caesar the things that are Caesar's, and to God the things that are God's. *And they were amazed at him.*

[65–B] And as for the dead being raised, have you not read in the book of Moses, in the passage about the bush, how God said to him, 'I am the God of Abraham, and the God of Isaac, and the God of Jacob'? He is not God of the dead, but of the living; you are quite wrong.

[66–B] *And Jesus said to him,* Do you see these great buildings? There will not be left here one stone upon another, that will not be thrown down.

[67–B] *But Jesus said,* Let her alone; why do you trouble her? She has done a beautiful thing to me. For you always have the poor with you, and whenever you will, you can do good to them; but you will not always have me. She has done what she could; she has anointed my body beforehand for burying. And truly, I say to you, wherever the gospel is preached in the whole world, what she has done will be told in memory of her.

[68–B] *He said to them,* It is one of the twelve, one who is dipping bread into the dish with me. For the Son of man goes as it is written of him, but woe to that man by whom the Son of man is betrayed! It would have been better for that man if he had not been born.

[69–B] *And he said to them,* This is my blood of the covenant, which is poured out for many. Truly, I say to you, I shall not drink again of the fruit of the vine until that day when I drink it new in the kingdom of God.

[70–B]   *And Jesus said to them*, You will all fall away; for it is written, 'I will strike the shepherd, and the sheep will be scattered.' But after I am raised up, I will go before you to Galilee.

[71–B]   Watch and pray that you may not enter into temptation; the spirit indeed is willing, but the flesh is weak.

[72–B]   *And Jesus said to them*, Have you come out as against a robber, with swords and clubs to capture me? Day after day I was with you in the temple teaching, and you did not seize me. But let the scriptures be fulfilled.

[73–B]   *And Jesus said*, I am; and you will see the Son of man seated at the right hand of Power, and coming with the clouds of heaven.

[74–B]   *And at the ninth hour Jesus cried with a loud voice*, E'lo-i, E'lo-i, la'ma sabach-tha'ni? *which means*, My God, my God, why hast thou forsaken me?

[75–C]   *And he said*, Assuredly, I say to you, no prophet is accepted in his own country.

[76–C]   *But Jesus answering them said*, Have you not even read this, what David did when he was hungry, he and those who were with him: how he went into the house of God, took and ate the showbread, and also gave some to those with him, which is not lawful for any but the priests to eat? *And He said to them*, The Son of Man is also Lord of the Sabbath.

[77–C] *Then He lifted up his eyes toward His disciples, and said*: Blessed are you poor, for yours is the kingdom of God. Blessed are you who hunger now, for you shall be filled. Blessed are you who weep now, for you shall laugh. Blessed are you when men hate you, and when they exclude you, and revile you, and cast out your name as evil, for the Son of Man's sake. Rejoice in that day and leap for joy! For indeed your reward is great in heaven, for in like manner their fathers did to the prophets.

[78–C] *Then He turned to the woman and said to Simon*, Do you see this woman? I entered your house; you gave Me no water for My feet, but she has washed My feet with her tears and wiped them with the hair of her head. You gave Me no kiss, but this woman has not ceased to kiss My feet since the time I came in. You did not anoint My head with oil, but this woman has anointed My feet with fragrant oil. Therefore I say to you, her sins, which are many, are forgiven, for she loved much. But to whom little is forgiven, the same loves little. *Then He said to her*, Your sins are forgiven.

[79–C] *But He turned and rebuked them, and said*, You do not know what manner of spirit you are of. For the Son of Man did not come to destroy men's lives but to save them.

[80–C] *Jesus said to him*, Let the dead bury their own dead, but you go and preach the kingdom of God.

[81–C] He who is not with Me is against Me, and he who does not gather with Me scatters. When an unclean spirit goes out of a man, he goes through dry places, seeking rest; and finding none, he says, 'I will return to my house from which I came.' And when he comes, he finds it swept and put in order. Then he goes and takes with him seven other spirits more wicked than himself, and they enter and dwell there; and the last state of that man is worse than the first.

[82–C]   And anyone who speaks a word against the Son of Man, it will be forgiven him; but to him who blasphemes against the Holy Spirit, it will not be forgiven. Now when they bring you to the synagogues and magistrates and authorities, do not worry about how or what you should answer, or what you should say. For the Holy Spirit will teach you in that very hour what you ought to say.

[83–C]   *And Jesus answered and said to them,* Do you suppose that these Galileans were worse sinners than all other Galileans, because they suffered such things? I tell you, no; but unless you repent you will all likewise perish.

[84–C]   If anyone comes to Me and does not hate his father and mother, wife and children, brothers and sisters, yes, and his own life also, he cannot be My disciple. And whoever does not bear his cross and come after Me cannot be My disciple.

[85–C]   *But Jesus called to Him and said,* Let the little children come to Me, and do not forbid them; for of such is the kingdom of God. Assuredly, I say to you, whoever does not receive the kingdom of God as a little child will by no means enter it.

[86–C]   *And He said to them,* How can they say that the Christ is the Son of David? Now David himself said in the Book of Psalms: 'The Lord said to my Lord, sit at My right hand, till I make Your enemies Your footstool.' Therefore David calls Him 'Lord'; how is He then his Son?

[87-C]   *So He said,* Truly I say to you that this poor widow has put in more than all; for all these out of their abundance have put in offerings for God, but she out of her poverty put in all the livelihood that she had.

[88-C]   Heaven and earth will pass away, but My words will by no means pass away.

[89-C]   *Then He said to them,* With fervent desire I have desired to eat this Passover with you before I suffer; for I say to you, I will no longer eat of it until it is fulfilled in the kingdom of God. *Then He took the cup, and gave thanks, and said,* Take this and divide it among yourselves; for I say to you, I will not drink of the fruit of the vine until the kingdom of God comes. *And He took bread, gave thanks and broke it, and gave it to them, saying,* This is My body which is given for you; do this in remembrance of Me. *Likewise He also took the cup after supper, saying,* This cup is the new covenant in My blood, which is shed for you. But behold, the hand of My betrayer is with Me on the table. And truly the Son of Man goes as it has been determined, but woe to that man by whom He is betrayed!

[90-C]   *Then He said to them,* But now, he who has a money bag, let him take it, and likewise a knapsack; and he who has no sword, let him sell his garment and buy one. For I say to you that this which is written must still be accomplished in Me: 'And He was numbered with the transgressors.' For the things concerning Me have an end.

[91-C]   *But Jesus said to him,* Judas, are you betraying the Son of Man with a kiss?

[92-C]   *Then Jesus said,* Father, forgive them, for they do not know what they do.

[93-C] Assuredly, I say to you, today you will be with Me in Paradise.

[94-C] Father, 'into Your hands I commit My spirit.'

[95-C] *Then He said to them,* O foolish ones, and slow of heart to believe in all that the prophets have spoken! Ought not the Christ to have suffered these things and to enter into His glory?

[96-C] Peace to you.

[97-C] *And He said to them,* Why are you troubled? And why do doubts arise in your hearts? Behold My hands and My feet, that it is I Myself. Handle Me and see, for a spirit does not have flesh and bones as you see I have.

[98-C] *Then He said to them,* These are the words which I spoke to you while I was still with you, that all things must be fulfilled which were written in the Law of Moses and the Prophets and the Psalms concerning Me.

[99-C] *Then He said to them,* Thus it is written, and thus it was necessary for the Christ to suffer and to rise from the dead the third day, and that repentance and remission of sins should be preached in His name to all nations, beginning at Jerusalem. And you are witnesses of these things.

[100-D] *Jesus answered her,* If you knew the gift of God, and who it is that is saying to you, 'Give me a drink,' you would have asked him, and he would have given you living water.

[101-D] Everyone who drinks of this water will thirst again, but whoever drinks of the water that I shall give him will never thirst;

the water that I shall give him will become in him a spring of water welling up to eternal life.

[102-D] *The woman said to him, 'I know that Messiah is coming (he who is called Christ); when he comes he will show us all things.'*
   Jesus said to her, I who speak to you am he.

[103-D] Unless you see signs and wonders you will not believe.

[104-D] *Jesus said to him,* Rise, take up your pallet, and walk.

[105-D] *Afterward Jesus found him in the temple, and said to him,* See, you are well! Sin no more, that nothing worse befall you.

[106-D] Truly, truly, I say to you, He who hears my word and believes him who sent me, has eternal life; he does not come into judgment, but has passed from death to life.

[107-D] Not that the testimony which I receive is from man; but I say this that you may be saved. He was a burning and shining lamp, and you were willing to rejoice for a while in his light. But the testimony which I have is greater than that of John; for the works which the Father has granted me to accomplish, these very works which I am doing, bear me witness that the Father has sent me.

[108-D] How can you believe, who receive glory from one another and do not seek the glory that comes from the only God? Do not think that I shall accuse you to the Father; it is Moses who accuses you, on whom you set your hope. If you believed Moses, you would believe me, for he wrote of me. But if you do not believe his writings, how will you believe my words?

[109–D]   *Then they said to him, 'What must we do, to be doing the works of God?'*

Jesus answered them, This is the work of God, that you believe in him whom he has sent.

[110–D]   *So Jesus said to them,* Truly, truly, I say to you, unless you eat the flesh of the Son of man and drink his blood, you have no life in you; he who eats my flesh and drinks my blood has eternal life, and I will raise him up at the last day. For my flesh is food indeed, and my blood is drink indeed. He who eats my flesh and drinks my blood abides in me, and I in him.

[111–D]   *Jesus answered them,* I did one deed, and you all marvel at it. Moses gave you circumcision (not that it is from Moses, but from the fathers), and you circumcise a man upon the sabbath. If on the sabbath a man receives circumcision, so that the law of Moses may not be broken, are you angry with me because on the sabbath I made a man's whole body well?

[112–D]   *Jesus looked up and said to her,* Woman, where are they? Has no one condemned you? *She said, 'No one, Lord.' And Jesus said,* Neither do I condemn you; go, and do not sin again.

[113–D]   *Again Jesus spoke to them, saying,* I am the light of the world; he who follows me will not walk in darkness, but will have the light of life.

[114–D]   *They said to him therefore, 'Where is your Father?' Jesus answered,* You know neither me nor my Father; if you knew me, you would know my Father also.

[115–D]   *Again he said to them,* I go away, and you will seek me and die in your sin; where I am going, you cannot come.

[116–D]   *Jesus then said to the Jews who had believed in him,* If you continue in my word, you are truly my disciples, and you will know the truth, and the truth will make you free.

[117–D]   Did I not tell you that if you would believe you would see the glory of God?

[118–D]   He who loves his life loses it, and he who hates his life in this world will keep it for eternal life.

[119–D]   What I am doing you do not know now, but afterward you will understand.

[120–D]   He who has bathed does not need to wash, except for his feet, but he is clean all over; and you are clean, but not every one of you.

[121–D]   For I have given you an example, that you also should do as I have done to you. Truly, truly, I say to you, a servant is not greater than his master; nor is he who is sent greater than he who sent him. If you know these things, blessed are you if you do them.

[122–D]   I am not speaking of you all; I know whom I have chosen; it is that the scripture may be fulfilled, 'He who ate my bread has lifted his heel against me.' I tell you this now, before it takes place, that when it does take place you may believe that I am he.

[123–D]   Little children, yet a little while I am with you. You will seek me; and as I said to the Jews so now I say to you, 'Where I am going you cannot come.'

[124–D]   Have I been with you so long, and yet you do not know me, Philip? He who has seen me has seen the Father; how can you say, 'Show us the Father'? Do you not believe that I am in the Father and the Father in me? The words that I say to you I do not speak on my own authority; but the Father who dwells in me does his works. Believe me that I am in the Father and the Father in me; or else believe me for the sake of the works themselves. Truly, truly, I say to you, he who believes in me will also do the works that I do; and greater works than these will he do, because I go to the Father. Whatever you ask in my name, I will do it, that the Father may be glorified in the Son; if you ask anything in my name, I will do it.

[125-D]   And I will pray the Father, and he will give you another Counselor, to be with you for ever, even the Spirit of truth, whom the world cannot receive, because it neither sees him nor knows him; you know him, for he dwells with you, and will be in you. I will not leave you desolate; I will come to you. Yet a little while, and the world will see me no more, but you will see me; because I live, you will live also. In that day you will know that I am in my Father, and you in me, and I in you.

[126-D]   Peace I leave with you; my peace I give to you; not as the world gives do I give to you. Let not your hearts be troubled, neither let them be afraid. You heard me say to you, 'I go away, and I will come to you.' If you loved me, you would have rejoiced, because I go to the Father; for the Father is greater than I. And now I have told you before it takes place, so that when it does take place, you may believe. I will no longer talk much with you, for the ruler of this world is coming. He has no power over me; but I do as the Father has commanded me, so that the world may know that I love the Father. Rise, let us go hence.

[127-D]   If you abide in me, and my words abide in you, ask whatever you will, and it shall be done for you. By this my Father is glorified, that you bear much fruit, and so prove to be my disciples. As the Father has loved me, so I have loved you; abide in my love. If you keep my commandments, you will abide in my love, just as I have kept my Father's commandments and abide in his love. These things I have spoken to you, that my joy may be in you, and that your joy may be full.

[128-D]   Remember the word that I said to you, 'A servant is not greater than his master.' If they persecuted me, they will persecute you; if they kept my word, they will keep yours also. But all this they will do to you on my account, because they do not know him who sent me. If I had not come and spoken to them, they would not have sin; but now they have no excuse for their sin.

[129-D]   If I had not done among them the works which no one else did, they would not have sin; but now they have seen and hated both me and my Father. It is to fulfill the word that is written in their law, 'They hated me without a cause.'

[130-D]   In that day you will ask nothing of me. Truly, truly, I say to you, if you ask anything of the Father, he will give it to you in my name.

[131-D]   *Jesus said to Peter,* Put your sword into its sheath; shall I not drink the cup which the Father has given me?

[132-D]   *Jesus answered,* My kingship is not of this world; if my kingship were of this world, my servants would fight, that I might not be handed over to the Jews; but my kingship is not from the world.
Pilate said to him, 'So you are a king?' Jesus answered, You say that I am a king. For this I was born, and for this I have come into the world, to bear witness to the truth. Every one who is of the truth hears my voice.

[133–D]   You would have no power over me unless it had been given you from above; therefore he who delivered me to you has the greater sin.

[134–D]   Do not hold me, for I have not yet ascended to the Father; but go to my brethren and say to them, I am ascending to my Father and your Father, to my God and your God.

[135–D]   *Jesus said to them again,* Peace be with you. As the Father has sent me, even so I send you. *And when he had said this, he breathed on them, and said to them,* Receive the Holy Spirit. If you forgive the sins of any, they are forgiven; if you retain the sins of any, they are retained.

[136–D]   *Jesus said to him,* Have you believed because you have seen me? Blessed are those who have not seen and yet believe.

[137–D]   Truly, truly, I say to you, when you were young, you girded yourself and walked where you would; but when you are old, you will stretch out your hands, and another will gird you and carry you where you do not wish to go.

[138–D]   *When Peter saw him, he said to Jesus, 'Lord, what about this man?' Jesus said to him,* If it is my will that he remain until I come, what is that to you? Follow me!

[139–F]   *These are the secret sayings which the living Jesus spoke and which Didymos Judas Thomas wrote down. And he said,* Whoever finds the interpretation of these sayings will not experience death.

[140–G]   . . . *we said to him, 'Have you departed and removed yourself from us?' But Jesus said,* No, but I shall go to the place from whence I came. If you wish to come with me, come!

[141–H]   You who have joined the perfect, the light, with the Holy Spirit, unite the angels with us also, the images.

[142–H]   *They said to him, 'Why do you love her more than all of us?' The Savior answered and said to them,* Why do I not love you like her?

[143–I]   *The Savior said,* Brother Thomas, while you have time in the world, listen to me and I will reveal to you the things you have pondered in your mind. Now since it has been said that you are my twin and true companion, examine yourself that you may understand who you are, in what way you exist, and how you will come to be. Since you are called my brother, it is not fitting that you be ignorant of yourself. And I know that you have understood, because you had already understood that I am the knowledge of the truth. So while you accompany me, although you are uncomprehending, you have (in fact) already come to know, and you will be called 'the one who knows himself.' For he who has not known himself has known nothing, but he who has known himself has at the same time already achieved knowledge about the Depth of the All. So then, you, my brother Thomas, have beheld what is obscure to men, that is, that against which they ignorantly stumble.

[144–J]   But they did not find him, nor was he mentioned among any generation of the prophets. He has now appeared among these, in him who appeared, who is the Son of Man who is exalted above the heavens in a fear of men of like essence. But you yourself, Peter, become perfect in accordance with your name with myself, the one who chose you, because from you I have established a base for the remnant whom I have summoned to knowledge. Therefore be strong until the imitation of righteousness — of him who had summoned you, having summoned you to know him in a way which is worth doing because of the rejection which happened to him, and sinews of his hands and his feet, and the crowning by those of the middle region, and the body of his radiance which they bring in hope of service because of a reward of honor — as he was about to reprove you three times in this night.

[145-J] *And he said to me,* Peter, I have told you many times that they are blind ones who have no guide. If you want to know their blindness, put your hands upon your eyes — your robe — and say what you see. *But when I had done it, I did not see anything. I said, 'No one sees this way.' Again he told me,* Do it again. *And there came in me fear with joy, for I saw a new light greater than the light of day. Then it came down upon the Savior. And I told him about those things which I saw. And he said to me again,* Lift up your hands and listen to what the priests and the people are saying. *And I listened to the priests as they sat with the scribes. The multitudes were shouting with their voice. When he heard these things from me he said to me,* Prick up your ears and listen to the things they are saying. *And I listened again. 'As you sit they are praising you.'*

[146-J] And still others of them who suffer think that they will perfect the wisdom of the brotherhood which really exists, which is the spiritual fellowship with those united in communion, through which the wedding of incorruptibility shall be revealed. The kindred race of the sisterhood will appear as an imitation. These are the ones who oppress their brothers, saying to them, 'Through this our God has pity, since salvation comes to us through this,' not knowing the punishment of those who are made glad by those who have done this thing to the little ones whom they saw, and whom they took prisoner.

[147-N] He is unnameable. He has no human form; for whoever has human form is the creation of another. And he has a semblance of his own — not like what you have seen or received, but a strange semblance that surpasses all things and is better than the universe. It looks to every side and sees itself from itself. Since it has no boundary, he is ever incomprehensible. He is imperishable, since he has no likeness to anything. He is unchanging good. He is faultless. He is eternal. He is blessed. While he is not known, he ever knows himself. He is immeasurable. He is untraceable. He is perfect, having no defect. He is imperishably blessed. He is called 'the Father of the Universe.'

[148-N]   I came from the Boundless One so that I might tell you all things. The Spirit That Exists was a begetter, who had a power of a begetting and form-giving being, so that the great abundance that was hidden in him might be revealed. Because of his mercy and his love he wished to bring forth fruit by himself, so that he might not enjoy his blessedness alone, but other spirits of the unwavering generation might bring forth body and fruit, glory and honor in imperishableness and his unending grace, so that his blessing might be revealed by the selfbegotten God, the Father of every imperishableness and those that came to be after them. But that which appears has not yet been arrived at.

[149-N]   Come from the non-appearing things to the completion of those that are revealed, and she, the effluence of thought, will reveal to you how the belief in those things that are not revealed was found in those that are revealed, those that belong to the Unbegotten Father. Whoever has an ear to hear, let him hear.

[150-O]   Let us gather an assembly together. Let us visit that creation of his. Let us send someone forth in it, just as he visited the Ennoias, the regions below. And I said these things to the whole multitude of the multitudinous assembly of the rejoicing Majesty.

The whole house of the Father of Truth rejoiced that I am the one who is from them. I produced thought about the Ennoias which came out of the undefiled Spirit, about the descent upon the water, that is, the regions below. And they all had a single mind, since it is out of one. They charged me since I was willing. I came forth to reveal the glory to my kindred and my fellow spirits.

For those who were in the world had been prepared by the work of our sister Sophia — she who is a whore — because of the innocence which has not been uttered. And she did not ask anything from the All, nor from the greatness of the Assembly, nor from the Pleroma. Since she was first she came forth to prepare monads and places for the Son of Light, and the fellow workers which she took from the elements below to build bodily dwellings from them. But, having come into being in an empty glory, they ended in destruction in the dwellings in which they were, since they were prepared by Sophia. They stand ready to receive the life-giving word of the ineffable Monad and of the greatness of the assembly of all those who persevere and those who are in me.

[151-O]   There was a great disturbance in the whole earthly area with confusion and flight, as well as in the plan of the archons. And some were persuaded, when they saw the wonders which were being accomplished by me. And all these, with the race, that came down, flee from him who had fled from the throne to the Sophia of hope, since she had earlier given the sign concerning us and all the ones with me — those of the race of Adonaios. Others also fled, as if from the Cosmocrator and those with him, since they have brought every kind of punishment upon me. And there was a flight of their mind about what they would counsel concerning me, thinking that she (Sophia) is the whole greatness, and speaking false witness, moreover, against the Man and the whole greatness of the assembly.

It was not possible for them to know who the Father of Truth, the Man of the Greatness, is. But they who received the name because of contact with ignorance — which is a burning and a vessel — having created it to destroy Adam whom they had made, in order to cover up those who are theirs in the same way. But they, the archons, those of the place of Yaldabaoth, reveal the realm of the angels, which humanity was seeking in order that they may not know the Man of Truth. For Adam, whom they had formed, appeared to them. And a fearful motion came about throughout their entire dwelling, lest the angels surrounding them rebel. For without those who were offering praise — I did not really die lest their archangel become empty.

[152-O]   And then a voice — of the Cosmocrator — came to the angels: 'I am God and there is no other beside me.' But I laughed joyfully when I examined his empty glory. But he went on to say, 'Who is man?' And the entire host of his angels who had seen Adam and his dwelling were laughing at his smallness. And thus did their Ennoia come to be removed outside the Majesty of the heavens, i.e. the Man of Truth, whose name they saw since he is in a small dwelling place, since they are small and senseless in their empty Ennoia, namely their laughter. It was contagion for them.

[153-O]   And the Son of the Majesty, who was hidden in the region below, we brought to the height here I was in all these aeons with them, which height no one has seen nor known, where the wedding of the wedding robe is, the new one and not the old, nor does it perish. For it is a new and perfect bridal chamber of the heavens, as I have revealed that there are three ways: an undefiled mystery in a spirit of this aeon, which does not perish, nor is it fragmentary, nor able to be spoken of; rather, it is undivided, universal, and permanent. For the soul, the one from the height, will not speak about the error which is here, nor transfer from these aeons, since it will be transferred when it becomes free and when it is endowed with nobility in the world, standing before the Father without weariness and fear, always mixed with the Nous of power and of form. They will see me from every side without hatred. For since they see me, they are being seen and are mixed with them. Since they did not put me to shame, they were not put to shame. Since they were not afraid before me, they will pass by every gate without fear and will be perfected in the third glory.

[154-O]   It was my going to the revealed height which the world did not accept, my third baptism in a revealed image. When they had fled from the fire of the seven Authorities, and the sun of the powers of the archons set, darkness took them. And the world become poor when he was restrained with a multitude of fetters. They nailed him to the tree, and they fixed him with four nails of brass. The veil of his temple he tore with his hands. It was a trembling which seized the chaos of the earth, for the souls which were in the sleep below were released. And they arose. They went about boldly, having shed zealous service of ignorance and unlearnedness beside the dead tombs, having put on the new man, since they have come to know that perfect Blessed One of the eternal and incomprehensible Father and the infinite light, which is I, since I came to my own and united them with myself. There is no need for many words, for our Ennoia was with their Ennoia. Therefore they knew what I speak of, for we took counsel about the destruction of the archons. And therefore I did the will of the Father, who is I.

[155-O]   For it was ludicrous. It is I who bear witness that it was ludicrous, since the archons do not know that it is an ineffable union of undefiled truth, as exists among the sons of light, of which they made an imitation, having proclaimed a doctine of a dead man and lies so as to resemble the freedom and purity of the perfect assembly, and joining themselves with their doctrine to fear and slavery, worldly cares, and abandoned worship, being small and ignorant since they do not contain the nobility of the truth, for they hate the one in whom they are, and love the one in whom they are not. For they did not know the Knowledge of the Greatness, that it is from above and from a fountain of truth, and that it is not from slavery and jealousy, fear and love of worldly matter. For that which is not theirs and that which is theirs they use fearlessly and freely. They do not desire because they have authority, and they have a law from themselves over whatever they will wish.

[156-O]   For Adam was a laughingstock, since he was made a counterfeit type of man by the Hebdomad, as if he had become stronger than I and my brothers. We are innocent with respect to him, since we have not sinned. And Abraham and Isaac and Jacob were a laughingstock, since they, the counterfeit fathers, were given a name by the Hebdomad, as if he had become stronger than I and my brothers. We are innocent with respect to him, since we have not sinned. David was a laughingstock in that his son was named the Son of Man, having been influenced by the Hebdomad, as if he had become stronger than I and the fellow members of my race. But we are innocent with respect to him; we have not sinned. Solomon was a laughingstock, since he thought that he was Christ, having become vain through the Hebdomad, as if he had become stronger than I and my brothers. But we are innocent with respect to him. I have not sinned. The 12 prophets were laughingstocks, since they have come forth as imitations of the true prophets. They came into being as counterfeits through the Hebdomad, as if he had become stronger than I and my brothers. But we are innocent with respect to him, since we have not sinned. Moses, a faithful servant, was a laughingstock, having been named 'the Friend,' since they perversely bore witness concerning him who never knew me. Neither he nor those before him, from Adam to Moses and John the Baptist, none of them knew me nor my brothers. For they had a doctrine of angels to observe dietary laws and bitter slavery, since they never knew truth, nor will they know it. For there is a great deception upon their soul making it impossible for them ever to find a Nous of freedom in order to know him, until they come to know the Son of Man. Now concerning my Father, I am he whom the world did not know, and because of this, it (the world) rose up against me and my brothers. But we are innocent with respect to him; we have not sinned.

[157-O] For the Archon was a laughingstock because he said, 'I am God, and there is none greater than I. I alone am the Father, the Lord, and there is no other beside me. I am a jealous God, who brings the sins of the fathers upon the children for three and four generations.' As if he had become stronger than I and my brothers! But we are innocent with respect to him, in that we have not sinned, since we mastered his teaching. Thus he was in an empty glory. And he does not agree with our Father. And thus through our fellowship we grasped his teaching, since he was vain in an empty glory. And he does not agree with our Father, for he was a laughingstock and judgment and false prophecy.

[158-O] Then before the foundation of the world, when the whole multitude of the Assembly came together upon the places of the Ogdoad, when they had taken counsel about a spiritual wedding which is in union, and thus he was perfected in the ineffable places by a living word, the undefiled wedding was consummated through the Mesotes of Jesus, who inhabits them all and possesses them, who abides in an undivided love of power. And surrounding him, he appears to him as a Monad of all these, a thought and a father, since he is one. And he stands by them all, since he as a whole came forth alone. And he is life, since he came from the Father of ineffable and perfect Truth, the father of those who are there, the union of peace and a friend of good things, and life eternal and undefiled joy, in a great harmony of life and faith, through eternal life of fatherhood and motherhood and sisterhood and rational wisdom. They had agreed with Nous, who stretches out and will stretch out in joyful union and is trustworthy and faithfully listens to someone. And he is in fatherhood and motherhood and rational brotherhood and wisdom. And this is a wedding of truth, and a repose of incorruption, in a spirit of truth, in every mind, and a perfect light in an unnameable mystery. But this is not, nor will it happen among us in any region or place in division and breach of peace, but in union and a mixture of love, all of which are perfected in the one who is.

[159–O]   But the archons around Yaldabaoth were disobedient because of the Ennoia who went down to him from her sister Sophia. They made for themselves a union with those who were with them in a mixture of a fiery cloud, which was their Envy, and the rest who were brought forth by their creatures, as if they had bruised the noble pleasure of the Assembly. And therefore they revealed a mixture of ignorance in a counterfeit of fire and earth and a murderer, since they are small and untaught, without knowledge having dared these things, and not having understood that light has fellowship with light, and darkness with darkness, and the corruptible with the perishable, and the imperishable with the incorruptible.

[160–U]   *And my Lord Jesus Christ, our King, said to me,* Let us go into the holy mountain. *And his disciples went with him, praying.*

IX

Apocalyptic and Revelation

[1–A]   The Son of man shall be betrayed into the hands of men: And they shall kill him, and the third day he shall be raised again.

[2–A]   *And Jesus said unto them,* See ye not all these things? Verily I say unto you, there shall not be left here one stone upon another, that shall not be thrown down.

[3–A]   Take heed that no man deceive you. For many shall come in my name, saying, I am Christ; and shall deceive many.

[4–A]   And ye shall hear of wars and rumors of wars: see that ye be not troubled: for all these things must come to pass, but the end is not yet. For nation shall rise against nation, and kingdom against kingdom: and there shall be famines, and pestilences, and earthquakes, in diverse places. All these are the beginning of sorrows.

[5–A] Then shall they deliver you up to be afflicted, and shall kill you: and ye shall be hated of all nations for my name's sake. And then shall many be offended, and shall betray one another, and shall hate one another.

[6–A] And many false prophets shall rise, and shall deceive many.

[7–A] And because iniquity shall abound, the love of many shall wax cold. But he that shall endure unto the end, the same shall be saved.

[8–A] And this gospel of the kingdom shall be preached in all the world for a witness unto all nations; and then shall the end come.

[9–A] When ye therefore shall see the abomination of desolation, spoken of by Daniel the prophet, stand in the holy place, (whoso readeth, let him understand): Then let them which be in Judaea flee unto the mountains: let him which is on the housetop not come down to take any thing out of his house: neither let him which is in the field return to take his clothes.

[10–A] And woe unto them that are with child, and to them that give suck in those days! But pray ye that your flight be not in the winter, neither on the sabbath day. For then shall be great tribulation, such as was not since the beginning of the world to this time, no, nor ever shall be. And except those days should be shortened, there should be no flesh saved: but for the elect's sake those days shall be shortened.

[11–A] Then if any man shall say unto you, Lo, here is Christ, or there; believe it not. For there shall arise false Christs, and false prophets, and shall show great signs and wonders; insomuch that, if it were possible, they shall deceive the very elect.

[12–A] Behold, I have told you before. Wherefore if they shall say unto you, behold, he is in the desert, go not forth; behold, he is in the secret chambers, believe it not. For as the lightning cometh out of the east, and shineth even unto the west; so shall also the coming of the Son of man be. For wheresoever the carcass is, there will the eagles be gathered together.

[13–A] Immediately after the tribulation of those days shall the sun be darkened and the moon shall not give her light, and the stars shall fall from heaven, and the powers of the heavens shall be shaken: and then shall appear the sign of the Son of man in heaven: and then shall the tribes of the earth mourn, and they shall see the Son of man coming in the clouds of heaven with power and great glory.

[14–A] And he shall send his angels with a great sound of a trumpet, and they shall gather together his elect from the four winds, from one end of heaven to the other.

[15–A] But of that day and hour knoweth no man, no, not the angels of heaven, nor the Son, but my Father only.

[16–A] But as the days of Noe were, so shall also the coming of the Son of man be. For as in the days that were before the flood they were eating and drinking, marrying and giving in marriage, until the day that Noe entered into the ark, And knew not until the flood came, and took them all away; so shall also the coming of the Son of man be.

[17–A] Then shall two be in the field; the one shall be taken, and the other left. Two women shall be grinding at the mill; the one shall be taken, and the other left.

[18-A]   Watch therefore: for ye know not what hour your Lord doth come. But know this, that if the goodman of the house had known in what watch the thief would come, he would have watched, and would not have suffered his house to be broken up. Therefore be ye also ready: for in such an hour as ye think not the Son of man cometh.

[19-A]   Who then is a faithful and wise servant, whom his lord hath made ruler over his household, to give them meat in due season? Blessed is that servant, whom his lord when he cometh shall find so doing. Verily I say unto you, that he shall make him ruler over all his goods. But and if that evil servant shall say in his heart, My lord delayeth his coming; And shall begin to smite his fellowservants, and to eat and drink with the drunken; The lord of that servant shall come in a day when he looketh not for him, and in an hour that he is not aware of, And shall cut him asunder, and appoint him his portion with the hypocrites: there shall be weeping and gnashing of teeth.

[20-A]   When the Son of man shall come in his glory, and all the holy angels with him, then shall he sit upon the throne of his glory: And before him shall be gathered all nations: and he shall separate them one from another, as a shepherd divideth his sheep from the goats: And he shall set the sheep on his right hand, but the goats on the left.

[21-A]   Then shall the King say unto them on his right hand, Come, ye blessed of my Father, inherit the kingdom prepared for you from the foundation of the world: For I was an hungered, and ye gave me meat: I was thirsty, and ye gave me drink: I was a stranger, and ye took me in: Naked, and ye clothed me: I was sick, and ye visited me: I was in prison, and ye came unto me. Then shall

the righteous answer him, saying, Lord, when saw we thee an hungred, and fed thee? or thirsty, and gave thee drink? When saw we
thee a stranger, and took thee in? or naked, and clothed thee? Or
when saw we thee sick, or in prison, and came unto thee? And the
King shall answer and say unto them, Verily, I say unto you, inasmuch as ye have done it unto one of the least of these my brethren,
ye have done it unto me.

[22–A]   Then shall he say also unto them on the left hand, Depart
from me, ye cursed, into everlasting fire, prepared for the devil and
his angels: For I was an hungred, and ye gave me no meat: I was
thirsty, and ye gave me no drink: I was a stranger, and ye took me
not in: naked, and ye clothed me not: sick, and in prison, and ye visited me not. Then shall they also answer him, saying, Lord, when
saw we thee hungred, or athirst, or a stranger, or naked, or sick, or
in prison, and did not minister unto thee? Then shall he answer
them, saying, Verily I say unto you, Inasmuch as ye did it not to one
of the least of these, ye did it not to me. And these shall go away into
everlasting punishment: but the righteous into life eternal.

[23–B]   *And Jesus began to say to them,* Take heed that no one leads
you astray. Many will come in my name, saying, 'I am he!' and they
will lead many astray.

[24–B]   And when you hear of wars and rumors of wars, do not be
alarmed; this must take place, but the end is not yet. For nation will
rise against nation, and kingdom against kingdom; there will be
earthquakes in various places, there will be famines; this is but the
beginning of the birth-pangs.

[25–B]   But take heed to yourselves: for they will deliver you up to
councils; and you will be beaten in synagogues; and you will stand

before governors and kings for my sake, to bear testimony before them. And the gospel must first be preached to all nations.

[26-B]   And when they bring you to trial and deliver you up, do not be anxious beforehand what you are to say; but say whatever is given you in that hour, for it is not you who speak, but the Holy Spirit.

[27-B]   And brother will deliver up brother to death, and the father his child, and children will rise against parents and have them put to death; and you will be hated by all for my name's sake. But he who endures to the end will be saved.

[28-B]   But when you see the desolating sacrilege set up where it ought not to be (let the reader understand), then let those who are in Judea flee to the mountains; let him who is on the housetop not go down, nor enter his house, to take anything away; and let him who is in the field not turn back to take his mantle.

[29-B]   And alas for those who are with child and for those who give suck in those days! Pray that it may not happen in winter.

[30-B]   For in those days there will be such tribulation as has not been from the beginning of the creation which God created until now, and never will be. And if the Lord had not shortened the days, no human being would be saved; but for the sake of the elect, whom he chose, he shortened the days.

[31-B]   And then if any one says to you, 'Look, here is the Christ!' or 'Look, there he is!' do not believe it. False Christs and false prophets will arise and show signs and wonders, to lead astray, if possible, the elect. But take heed; I have told you all things beforehand.

[32–B]   But in those days, after that tribulation, the sun will be darkened, and the moon will not give its light, and the stars will be falling from heaven, and the powers in the heavens will be shaken. And then they will see the Son of man coming in clouds with great power and glory. And then he will send out the angels, and gather his elect from the four winds, from the ends of the earth to the ends of heaven.

[33–B]   But of that day or that hour no one knows, not even the angels in heaven, nor the Son, but only the Father. Take heed, watch; for you do not know when the time will come.

[34–B]   Watch therefore — for you do not know when the master of the house will come, in the evening, or at midnight, or at cockcrow, or in the morning — lest he come suddenly and find you alseep. And what I say to you I say to all: Watch.

[35–C]   The kingdom of God does not come with observation; nor will they say, 'See here!' or 'See there!' For indeed, the kingdom of God is within you.

[36–C]   The days will come when you will desire to see one of the days of the Son of Man, and you will not see it. And they will say to you, 'Look here!' or 'Look there!' Do not go after them or follow them.

[37–C]   For as the lightning that flashes out of one part under heaven shines to the other part under heaven, so also the Son of Man will be in His day. But first He must suffer many things and be rejected by this generation.

[38–C]   And as it was in the days of Noah, so it will be also in the days of the Son of man: They ate, they drank, they married wives, they were given in marriage, until the day that Noah entered the ark, and the flood came and destroyed them all. Likewise as it was also in the days of Lot: They ate, they drank, they bought, they sold, they planted, they built; but on the day that Lot went out of Sodom it rained fire and brimstone from heaven and destroyed them all. Even so will it be in the day when the Son of Man is revealed.

[39-C] In that day, he who is on the housetop, and his goods are in the house, let him not come down to take them away. And likewise the one who is in the field, let him not turn back. Remember Lot's wife.

[40-C] I tell you, in that night there will be two men in one bed: the one will be taken and the other will be left. Two women will be grinding together: the one will be taken and the other left. Two men will be in the field: the one will be taken and the other left.

[41-C] These things which you see — the days will come in which not one stone shall be left upon another that shall not be thrown down.

[42-C] Take heed that you not be decieved. For many will come in My name, saying, 'I am He,' and 'The time has drawn near.' Therefore do not go after them. But when you hear of wars and commotions, do not be terrified; for these things must come to pass first, but the end will not come immediately.

[43-C] Nation will rise against nation, and kingdom against kingdom. And there will be great earthquakes in various places, and famines and pestilences; and there will be fearful sights and great signs from heaven.

[44-C]   But before all these things, they will lay their hands on you and persecute you, delivering you up to the synagogues and prisons. You will be brought before kings and rulers for My name's sake. But it will turn out for you as an occasion for testimony. Therefore settle it in your hearts not to meditate beforehand on what you will answer; for I will give you a mouth and wisdom which all your adversaries will not be able to contradict or resist.

[45-C]   You will be betrayed even by parents and brothers, relatives and friends; and they will put some of you to death. And you will be hated by all for My name's sake. But not a hair of your head shall be lost. By your patience possess your souls.

[46-C]   But when you see Jerusalem surrounded by armies, then know that its desolation is near. Then let those who are in Judea flee to the mountains, let those who are in the midst of her depart, and let not those who are in the country enter her. For these are the days of vengeance, that all things which are written may be fulfilled.

[47-C]   But woe to those who are pregnant and to those who are nursing babies in those days! For there will be great distress in the land and wrath upon this people. And they will fall by the edge of the sword, and be led away captive into all nations. And Jerusalem will be trampled by Gentiles until the times of the Gentiles are fulfilled.

[48-C]   And there will be signs in the sun, in the moon, and in the stars; and on the earth distress of nations, with perplexity, the sea and the waves roaring; men's hearts failing them from fear and the expectation of those things which are coming on the earth, for the powers of the heavens will be shaken.

[49-C]   Then they will see the Son of Man coming in a cloud with power and great glory. Now when these things begin to happen, look up and lift up your heads, because your redemption draws near.

[50-C]   Look at the fig tree, and all the trees. When they are already budding, you see and know for yourselves that summer is now near. So you also, when you see these things happening, know that the kingdom of God is near.

[51-C]   But take heed to yourselves, lest your hearts be weighed down with carousing, drunkenness, and cares of this life, and that Day come on you unexpectedly. For it will come as a snare on all those who dwell on the face of the whole earth.

[52-D]   I have said all this to you to keep you from falling away. They will put you out of the synagogues; indeed, the hour is coming when whoever kills you will think he is offering service to God. And they will do this because they have not known the Father, nor me.

[53-D]   Nevertheless I tell you the truth: it is to your advantage that I go away, for if I do not go away, the Counselor will not come to you; but if I go, I will send him to you. And when he comes, he will convince the world concerning sin and righteousness and judgment: concerning sin, because they do not believe in me; concerning righteousness, because I go to the Father, and you will see me no more; concerning judgment, because the ruler of this world is judged.

[54-D]   I have yet many things to say to you, but you cannot bear them now. When the Spirit of truth comes, he will guide you into all the truth; for he will not speak on his own authority, but whatever he hears he will speak, and he will declare to you the things that are to come. He will glorify me, for he will take what is mine and declare it to you.

[55–D]   Truly, truly, I say to you, you will weep and lament, but the world will rejoice; you will be sorrowful, but your sorrow will turn into joy. When a woman is in travail she has sorrow, because her hour has come; but when she is delivered of the child, she no longer remembers the anguish, for joy that a child is born into the world. So you have sorrow now, but I will see you again and your hearts will rejoice, and no one will take your joy from you.

[56–E]   I know thy works, and thy labor, and thy patience, and how thou canst not bear them which are evil: and thou hast tried them which say they are apostles, and are not, and hast found them liars: And hast borne, and hast patience, and for my name's sake hast labored, and hast not fainted.

[57–E]   Nevertheless I have somewhat against thee, because thou hast left thy first love. Remember therefore from whence thou art fallen, and repent, and do the first works; or else I will come unto thee quickly, and will remove thy candlestick out of his place, except thou repent.

[58–E]   But this thou hast, that thou hatest the deeds of the Nicolaitanes, which I also hate. He that hath an ear, let him hear what the Spirit saith unto the churches; to him that overcometh will I give to eat of the tree of life, which is in the midst of the paradise of God.

[59–E]   And unto the angel of the church in Smyrna write, These things saith the first and the last, which was dead, and is alive; I know thy works, and tribulation, and poverty, (but thou art rich) and I know the blasphemy of them which say they are Jews, and are not, but are the synagogue of Satan.

[60-E]   Fear none of those things which thou shalt suffer; behold, the devil shall cast some of you into prison, that ye may be tried; and ye shall have tribulation ten days: be thou faithful unto death, and I will give thee a crown of life. He that hath an ear, let him hear what the Spirit saith unto the churches. He that overcometh shall not be hurt of the second death.

[61-E]   And to the angel of the church on Pergamos write; These things saith he which hath the sharp sword with two edges; I know thy works and where thou dwellest, even where Satan's seat is: and thou holdest fast my name, and hast not denied my faith, even in those days wherein Antipas was my faithful martyr, who was slain among you, where Satan dwelleth.

[62-E]   But I have a few things against thee, because thou hast there them that hold the doctrine of Balaam, who taught Balac to cast a stumbling block before the children of Israel, to eat things sacrificed unto idols, and to commit fornication. So hast thou also them that hold the doctrine of the Nicolaitanes, which thing I hate. Repent; or else I will come unto thee quickly, and will fight against them with the sword of my mouth.

[63-E]   He that hath an ear, let him hear what the Spirit saith unto the churches; To him that overcometh will I give to eat of the hidden manna, and will give him a white stone, and in the stone a new name written, which no man knoweth saving he that receiveth it.

[64-E]   And unto the angel of the church in Thyatira write; These things saith the Son of God, who hath his eyes like unto a flame of fire, and his feet are like fine brass; I know thy works, and charity, and service, and faith, and thy patience, and thy works; and the last to be more than the first.

[65-E] Notwithstanding I have a few things against thee, because thou sufferest that woman Jezebel, which calleth herself a prophetess, to teach and to seduce my servants to commit fornication, and to eat things sacrificed unto idols. And I gave her space to repent of her fornication; and she repented not. Behold, I will cast her into a bed, and them that commit adultery with her into great tribulation, except they repent of their deeds. And I will kill her children with death; and all the churches shall know that I am he which searcheth the reins and hearts: and I will give unto every one of you according to your works.

[66-E] But unto you I say, and unto the rest in Thyatira, as many as have not this doctrine, and which have not known the depths of Satan, as they speak, I will put upon you none other burden.

[67-E] But that which ye have already hold fast till I come. And he that overcometh, and keepeth my words unto the end, to him will I give power over the nations: And he shall rule them with a rod of iron: as the vessels of a potter shall they be broken to shivers: even as I received of my Father. And I will give him the morning star.

[68-E] And unto the angel of the church in Sardis write; These things saith he that hath the seven Spirits of God, and the seven stars; I know thy works, that thou hast a name that thou livest, and art dead.

[69-E] Be watchful, and strengthen the things which remain, that are ready to die: for I have not found thy works perfect before God.

[70–E]   Remember therefore how thou hast received and heard, and hold fast, and repent. If therefore thou shalt not watch, I will come on thee as a thief, and thou shalt not know what hour I will come upon thee.

[71–E]   Thou hast a few names even in Sardis which have not defiled their garments; and they shall walk with me in white; for they are worthy. He that overcometh, the same shall be clothed in white raiment; and I will not blot out his name out of the book of life, but I will confess his name before my Father, and before his angels. He that hath an ear, let him hear what the Spirit saith unto the churches.

[72–E]   And to the angel of the church in Philadelphia write; These things saith he that is holy, he that is true, he that hath the key of David, he that openeth, and no man shutteth; and shutteth, and no man openeth; I know thy works: behold, I have set before thee an open door, and no man can shut it: for thou hast a little strength, and hast kept my word, and hast not denied my name.

[73–E]   Behold, I will make them of the synagogue of Satan, which say they are Jews, and are not, but do lie; behold, I will make them to come and worship before thy feet, and to know that I have loved thee. Because thou hast kept the word of my patience, I also will keep thee from the hour of temptation, which shall come upon all the world, to try them that dwell upon the earth.

[74–E]   Behold, I come quickly: hold that fast which thou hast, that no man take thy crown.

[75–E]   Him that overcometh will I make a pillar in the temple of my God, and he shall go no more out: and I will write upon him the name of my God, and the name of the city of my God, which is new Jerusalem, which cometh down out of heaven from my God: and I will write upon him my new name. He that hath an ear, let him hear what the Spirit saith unto the churches.

[76–E]   And unto the angel of the church of the Laodiceans write; These things saith the Amen, the faithful and true witness, the beginning of the creation of God; I know thy works, that thou art neither cold nor hot: I would thou wert cold or hot. So then because thou art lukewarm, and neither cold nor hot, I will spue thee out of my mouth.

[77–E]   Because thou sayest, I am rich, and increased with goods, and have need of nothing; and knowest not that thou art wretched, and miserable, and poor, and blind, and naked: I counsel thee to buy of me gold tried in the fire, that thou mayest be rich; and white raiment, that thou mayest be clothed, and that the shame of thy nakedness do not appear; and anoint thine eyes with eyesalve, that thou mayest see.

[78–E]   As many as I love, I rebuke and chasten: be zealous therefore, and repent. Behold, I stand at the door, and knock: if any man hear my voice, and open the door, I will come in to him, and will sup with him, and he with me.

[79–E]   To him that overcometh will I grant to sit with me in my throne, even as I also overcame, and am set down with my Father in his throne. He that hath an ear, let him hear what the Spirit saith unto the churches.

[80–F]   *The disciples said to Jesus, 'Tell us how our end will be.' Jesus said*, Have you discovered, then, the beginning, that you look for the end? For where the beginning is, there will the end be. Blessed is he who will take his place in the beginning; he will know the end and will not experience death.

[81–F] *Jesus said*, Two will rest on a bed: the one will die, and other will live.

Salome said, 'Who are You, man, that You, as though from the One, (or: as whose son), that You have come up on my couch and eaten from my table?'

Jesus said to her, I am he who exists from the Undivided. I was given some of the things of my father.

Salome said, 'I am your disciple.'

Jesus said to her, Therefore I say, if he is undivided, he will be filled with light, but if he is divided, he will be filled with darkness.

[82–F] *A woman from the crowd said to Him, 'Blessed are the womb which bore you and the breasts which nourished you.'*

He said to her, Blessed are those who have heard the word of the Father and have truly kept it. For there will be days when you will say, 'Blessed are the womb which has not conceived and the breasts which have not given milk.'

[83–F] *Jesus said*, The heavens and the earth will be rolled up in your presence. And the one who lives from the Living One will not see death. *Does not Jesus say*, Whoever finds himself is superior to the world?

[84–F] *His disciples said to him, 'When will the Kingdom come?'*

Jesus said, It will not come by waiting for it. It will not be a matter of saying 'Here it is' or 'There it is.' Rather, the Kingdom of the Father is spread out upon the earth, and men do not see it.

[85-J]   For many will accept our teaching in the beginning. And they will turn from them again by the will of the Father of their error, because they have done what he wanted. And he will reveal them in his judgment, i.e. the servants of the Word. But those who became mingled with these shall become their prisoners, since they are without perception. And the guileless, good, pure one they push to the worker of death, and to the kingdom of those who praise Christ in a restoration. And they praise the men of the propagation of falsehood, those who will come after you. And they will cleave to the name of a dead man, thinking that they will become pure. But they will become greatly defiled and they will fall into a name of error, and into the hand of an evil, cunning man and a manifold dogma, and they will be ruled heretically.

For some of them will blaspheme the truth and proclaim evil teaching. And they will say evil things against each other. Such will be named: those who stand in the strength of the archons, of a man and a naked woman who is manifold and subject to much suffering. And those who say these things will ask about dreams. And if they say that a dream came from a demon worthy of their error, then they shall be given perdition instead of incorruption.

[86-J]   But many others, who oppose the truth and are the messengers of error, will set up their error and their law against these pure thoughts of mine, as looking out from one perspective, thinking that good and evil are from one source. They do business in my word. And they will propagate harsh fate. The race of immortal souls will go in it in vain until my Parousia. For they shall come out of them — and my forgiveness of their transgressions into which they fell through their adversaries, whose ransom I got from the slavery in which they were, to give them freedom that they may create an imitation remnant in the name of a dead man, who is Hermas, of the first-born of unrighteousness, in order that the light which exists may not be believed by the little ones. But those of this sort are the workers who will be cast into the outer darkness, away from the sons of light. For neither will they enter, nor do they permit those who are going up to their approval for their release.

[87–J] And still others of them who suffer think that they will perfect the wisdom of the brotherhood which really exists, which is the spiritual fellowship with those united in communion, through which the wedding of incorruptibility shall be revealed. The kindred race of the sisterhood will appear as an imitation. These are the ones who oppress their brothers, saying to them, 'Through this our God has pity, since salvation comes to us through this,' not knowing the punishment of those who are made glad by those who have done this thing to the little ones whom they saw, and whom they took prisoner.

[88–J] Come therefore, let us go on with the completion of the will of the incorruptible Father. For behold, those who will bring them judgment are coming, and they will put them to shame. But me they cannot touch. And you, O Peter, shall stand in their midst. Do not be afraid because of your cowardice. Their minds shall be closed, for the invisible one has opposed them.

[89–Q] *And we said to him, 'O Lord, how many years yet?' And he said to us,* When the hundred and fiftieth year is completed, between Pentecost and Passover will the coming of my Father take place.

[90–Q] You will see a light brighter than light and more perfect than perfection. And the Son will be perfected through the Father, the light — for the Father is perfect (the Son) whom death and resurrection make perfect, and the one accomplishment surpasses the other. And I am fully the right hand of the Father; I am in him who accomplishes.

[91–Q]   Have confidence and be of good courage. Truly I say to you, such a rest will be yours where there is no eating and drinking and no mourning and singing (or care) and neither earthly garment nor perishing. And you will not have part in the creation of below, but will belong to the incorruptibility of my Father, you who will not perish. As I am continually in the Father, so also you are in me.

[92–Q]   *Then he said to us,* Does the flesh or the spirit fall away? *And we said to him, 'The flesh.' And he said to us,* Now what has fallen will arise, and what is ill will be sound, that my Father may be praised therein; as he has done to me, so I will do to you and to all who believe in me. Truly I say to you, the flesh will rise alive with the soul, that they may confess and be judged with the work they have done, whether it is good or bad, in order that it may become a selection and exhibition for those who have believed and have done the commandment of my Father who sent me. Then will the righteous judgment take place; for thus my Father wills, and he said to me, 'My son, on the day of Judgment you will not fear the rich and not spare the poor; rather deliver each one to eternal punishment according to his sins.' But to those who have loved me and do love me and who have done my commandment I will grant rest in life in the kingdom of my heavenly Father. Look, see what kind of power he has granted me, and he has given me, that . . . what I want and as I have wanted . . . and in whom I have awakened hope.

[93–Q]   *And he said to us,* As those who fulfill what is good and beautiful, so the wicked shall be manifest. And then a righteous judgment will take place according to their work, how they have acted; and they will be delivered to ruin.

[94–Q]   There is coming a time and an hour when it is in store for you to go to your Father.

[95-Q] And look; you will meet a man whose name is Saul, which being interpreted means Paul. He is a Jew, circumcised according to the command of the law; and he will hear my voice from heaven with terror, fear, and trembling; and his eyes will be darkened and by your hand be crossed with spittle. And do all to him as I have done to you. Deliver (?) (him?) to others. And this man — immediately his eyes will be opened, and he will praise God, my heavenly Father. And he will become strong among the nations and will preach and teach, and many will be delighted when they hear and will be saved. Then will he be hated and delivered into the hand of his enemy, and he will testify before mortal kings, and upon him will come the completion of the testimony to me; because he had persecuted and hated me, he will be converted to me and preach and teach, and he will be among my elect, a chosen vessel and a wall that does not fall. The last of the last will become a preacher to the Gentiles, perfect in the will of my Father. As you have learned from the Scriptures that your fathers the prophets spoke concerning me, and it is fulfilled in me — *this certain thing he said* — so you must become a leader to them. And every word which I have spoken to you and which you have written concerning me, that I am the word of the Father and Father is in me, so you must become also to that man, as it befits you. Teach and remind him what has been said in the Scriptures and fulfilled concerning me, and then he will be for the salvation of the Gentiles.

[96-Q] *And we said again to him, 'When, Lord, will we meet that man, and when will you go to your Father and to our God and Lord?' And he answered and said to us,* That man will set out from the land of Cilicia to Damascus in Syria to tear asunder the Church which you must create. It is I who will speak to him through you, and he will come quickly. He will be strong in his faith, that the word of the prophet may be fulfilled where it says, 'Behold, out of the land of Syria I will begin to call a new Jerusalem, and I will subdue Zion and it will be captured; and the barren one who has no children will be fruitful and will be called the daughter of my Father, but to me, my bride; for so has it pleased him who sent me.' But that man will I turn aside, that he may not go there and complete his evil plan. And glory of my Father will come in through him. For after I have gone away and remain with my Father, I will speak with him from heaven; and it will all happen as I have predicted to you concerning him.

[97-Q] *And he said to us,* I will teach you, and not only what will happen to you, but also to those whom you shall teach and who shall believe; and there are such as will hear this man and will believe in me. In those years and in those days this will happen.

And we said to him again, 'O Lord, what is it then that will happen?'

And he said to us, Then will the believers and also they who do not believe see a trumpet in heaven, and the sight of great stars that are visible while it is day, and a dragon reaching from heaven to earth, and stars that are like fire falling down and great hailstones of severe fire; and how sun and moon fight against each other, and constantly the frightening of thunder and lightning, thunderclaps and earthquakes, how cities fall down and in their ruin men die, constant drought from the failing of the rain, a great plague and an extensive and often quick death, so that those who die will lack a grave; and the going out of children and relatives will be on one bed (or, bier). And the relative will not turn toward his child, nor the child to his relative; and a man will not turn toward his neighbor. But those forsaken who were left behind will rise up and see those who forsook them when they brought them out because there was plague. Everything is hatred and affliction and jealousy, and they will take from the one and give to another; and what comes after this will be worse than this.

[98-Q]   Then my Father will become angry because of the wickedness of men; for their offenses are many and the horror of their impurity is much against them in the corruption of their life. *And we said to him, 'What, Lord, what is allotted to those who hope in you?' And he answered and said to us,* How long are you still slow of heart? Truly I say to you, as the prophet David has spoken concerning me and my people, so will it also be concerning those who shall believe in me. But there will be in the world deceivers and enemies of righteousness, and they will meet the prophecy of David who said, 'Their feet are quick to shed blood and their tongue weaves deceit, and the venom of serpents is under their lips. And I see you as you wander with a thief and your share is with a fornicator. While you sit there furthermore you slander your brother, and set a trap for the son of your mother. What do you think? Should I be like you?' And now see how the prophet of God has spoken concerning everything, that all may be fulfilled that was said before.

[99-Q]   *And we said to him, 'Will their exit from the world take place through a plague that has tormented them?' And he said to us,* No, but if they suffer torment, such suffering will be a test for them, whether they have faith and whether they keep in mind these words of mine and obey my commandment. They will rise up, and their waiting will last only a few days, that he who sent me may be glorified, and I with him. For he has sent me to you. I tell you this. But you tell it to Israel and to the Gentiles, that they may hear; they also are to be saved and believe in me and escape the distress of the plague. And whoever has escaped the distress of death, such a one will be taken and kept in prison, under torture like that of a thief.

[100-Q]   *And we said to him, 'O Lord, teach us what will happen after this.' And he said to us,* In those years and days there shall be war upon war, and the four corners of the world will be shaken and will make war upon each other. And then a disturbance of the clouds will take place, darkness and drought and persecution of those who believe in me, and of the elect. Then dissension, conflict, and evil of action against each other. Among them there are some who believe in my name and yet follow evil and teach vain teaching. And men will follow them and will submit themselves to their riches, their depravity, their mania for drinking, and their gifts of bribery; and respect of persons will rule among them.

[101–Q]   *And we said to him, 'O Lord, will all this happen?' And he said to us,* How will the judgment of righteousness take place for the sinners and the righteous? *And we said to him, 'Will they not in that day say to you, "You caused to lead toward righteousness and sin and have separated darkness and light, evil and good?"'*

[102–Q]   There will come another teaching and a conflict; and in that they seek their own glory and produce worthless teaching an offense of death will come thereby, and they will teach and turn away from my commandment even those who believe in me and bring them out of eternal life.

[103]–T Hearken, Thomas, for I am the Son of God the Father and I am the father of all spirits. Hear from me the signs which will be at the end of this world, when the end of the world will be fulfilled before my elect come forth from the world. I tell you openly what now is about to happen to men. When these are to take place the princes of the angels do not know, for they are now hidden from them. Then the kings will divide the world among themselves; there will be great hunger, great pestilences, and much distress on the earth. The sons of men will be enslaved in every nation and will perish by the sword. There will be great disorder on earth. Thereafter when the hour of the end draws near there will be great signs in the sky

for seven days and the powers of the heavens will be set in motion. Then at the beginning of the third hour of the first day there will be a mighty and strong voice in the firmament of the heaven; a cloud of blood will go up from the north and there will follow it great rolls of thunder and powerful flashes of lightning and it will cover the whole heaven. Then it will rain blood on all the earth. These are the signs of the first day.

[104-T]   And on the second day a great voice will resound in the firmament of heaven and the earth will be moved from its place. The gates of heaven will be opened in the firmament of heaven from the east. The smoke of a great fire will burst forth through the gates of heaven and will cover the whole heaven as far as the west. In that day there will be fears and great terrors in the world. These are the signs of the second day.

[105-T]   And on the third day at about the third hour there will be a great voice in heaven and the depths of the earth will roar out from the four corners of the world. The pinnacles of the firmament of heaven will be laid open and all the air will be filled with pillars of smoke. An exceedingly evil stench of sulphur will last until the tenth hour. Men will say: We think the end is upon us so that we perish. These are the signs of the third day.

[106-T]   And at the first hour of the fourth day the Abyss will melt and rumble from the land of the east; then the whole earth will shake before the force of the earthquake. In that day the idols of the heathen will fall as well as all the buildings of the earth before the force of the earthquake. These are the signs of the fourth day.

[107-T]   But on the fifth day at the sixth hour suddenly there will be great thunderings in the heaven and the powers of the light will flash and the sphere of the sun will be burst and great darkness will be in the whole world as far as the west. The air will be sorrowful without sun and moon. The stars will cease their work. In that day all nations will so see as if they were enclosed in a sack, and they will despise the life of this world. These are the signs of the fifth day.

[108–T]   And at the fourth hour of the sixth day there will be a great voice in heaven. The firmament of heaven will be split from east to west and the angels of the heavens will look out on the earth through the rents in the heavens and all men who are on earth will see the angelic host looking out from heaven. Then all men will flee into the tombs and hide themselves from before the righteous angels, and say, 'Oh that the earth would open and swallow us.' For such things will happen as never happened since this world was created. Then they will see me as I come down from above in the light of my Father with the power and honor of the holy angels. Then at my arrival the restraint on the fire of paradise will be loosed, for paradise is enclosed with fire. And this is the eternal fire which devours the earthly globe and all the elements of the world. Then the spirits and souls of the saints will come forth from paradise and come into all the earth, and each go to its own body where it is laid up; and each of them will say, 'Here my body is laid up.' And when the great voice of those spirits is heard there will be an earthquake everywhere in the earth and by the force of the earthquake the mountains will be shattered above and the rocks beneath. Then each spirit will return to its own vessel and the bodies of the saints who sleep will rise. Then their bodies will be changed into the image and likeness and honor of the holy angels and into the power of the image of my holy Father. Then they will put on the garment of eternal life: the garment from the cloud of light which has never been seen in this world; for this cloud comes down from the upper kingdom of the heavens by the power of my Father, and will invest with its glory every spirit that has believed in me. Then they will be clothed and, as I said to you before, borne by the hands of the holy angels. Then they will be carried off in a cloud of light into the air, and rejoicing go with me into the heavens and remain in the light and honor of my Father. Then there will be great joy for them in the presence of my Father and in the presence of the holy angels. These are the signs of the sixth day.

[109–T]   And at the eighth hour of the seventh day there will be voices in the four corners of Heaven. All the air will be set in motion and filled with holy angels. These will make war among themselves for the whole day. In that day the elect will be delivered by the holy angels from the destruction of the world. Then all men will see that the hour of their destruction is come near. These are the signs of the seventh day.

[110–T]   And when the seven days are finished, on the eighth day at the sixth hour there will be a gentle and pleasant voice in heaven from the east. Then that angel who has power over the holy angels will be made manifest. And there will go forth with him all the angels sitting on my holy Father's chariots of clouds, rejoicing and flying around in the air under heaven, to deliver the elect who believed in me; and they will rejoice that the destruction of the world has come. *The words of the Savior to Thomas about the end of this world are finished.*

[111–U]   *And our Lord answered and said unto us,* Take heed that men deceive you not and that ye do not become doubters and serve other gods. Many will come in my name saying 'I am Christ.' Believe them not and draw not near unto them. For the coming of the son of God will not be manifest, but like the lightning which shineth from the east to the west, so shall I come on the clouds of heaven with a great host in my glory; with my cross going before my face will I come in my glory, shining seven times as bright as the sun will I come in my glory, with all my saints, my angels, when my Father will place a crown upon my head, that I may judge the living and the dead and recompense every man according to his work. And ye, receive ye the parable of the fig-tree thereon: as soon a its shoots have gone forth and its boughs have sprouted, the end of the world will come.

[112–U]   Hast thou not grasped that the fig-tree is the house of Israel? Verily, I say to you, when its boughs have sprouted at the end, then shall deceiving Christs come, and awaken hope with the words: 'I am the Christ, who am now come into the world.' And when they shall see the wickedness of their deeds even of the false Christs, they shall turn away after them and deny him to whom our fathers gave praise, the first Christ whom they crucified and thereby sinned exceedingly. But this deceiver is not the Christ. And when they reject him, he will kill with the sword and there shall be many martyrs. Then shall the boughs of the fig-tree, i.e. the house of Israel, sprout, and there shall be many martyrs by his hand: they shall be killed and become martyrs. Enoch and Elias will be sent to instruct them that this is the deceiver who must come into the world and do signs and wonders in order to deceive. And therefore shall they that are slain by his hand be martyrs and shall be reckoned among the good and righteous martyrs who have pleased God in their life.

[113–U]   Behold now what they shall experience in the last days, when the day of God comes. On the day of the decision of the judgment of God, all the children of men from the east unto the west shall be gathered before my Father who ever liveth, and he will command hell to open its bars of steel and to give up all that is in it.

And the beasts and fowls shall he command to give back all flesh that they have devoured, since he desires that men should appear again; for nothing perishes for God, and nothing is impossible with him, since all things are his. For all things come to pass on the day of decision, on the day of judgment, at the word of God, and as all things came to pass when he created the world and commanded all that is therein, and it was all done — so shall it be in the last days; for everything is possible with God and he says in the Scripture: 'Son of man, prophesy upon the several bones, and say to the bones — bone unto bone in joints, sinews, nerves, flesh and skin and hair thereon.' And soul and spirit shall the great Uriel give at the command of God. For him God has appointed over the resurrection of the dead on the day of judgment.

[114–U]   And these things shall come to pass in the day of judgment of those who have fallen away from faith in God and have committed sin: cataracts of fire shall be let loose; and obscurity and darkness shall come up and cover and veil the entire world, and the waters shall be changed and transformed into coals of fire, and all that is in it shall burn and the sea shall become fire; under the heaven there shall be a fierce fire that shall not be put out and it flows for the judgment of wrath. And the stars shall be melted by flames of fire, as if they had not been created, and the fastnesses of heaven shall pass away for want of water and become as though they had not been created. And the lightnings of heaven shall be no more and, by their enchantment, they shall alarm the world. And the spirits of the dead bodies shall be like to them and at the command of God will become fire. And as soon as the whole creation is dissolved, the men who are in the east shall flee to the west and those in the west to the east; those that are in the south shall flee to the north and those in the north to the south, and everywhere will the wrath of the fearful fire overtake them; and an unquenchable flame shall drive them and bring them to the judgment of wrath in the stream of unquenchable fire which flows, flaming with fire, and when its waves separate one from another, seething, there shall be much gnashing of teeth among the children of men.

[115–U]   And all will see how I come upon an eternal shining cloud, and the angels of God who will sit with me on the throne of my glory at the right hand of my heavenly Father. He will set a crown upon my head. As soon as the nations see it, they will weep, each nation for itself. And he shall command them to go into the river of fire, while the deeds of each individual one of them stand before him. Recompense shall be given to each according to his work. As for the elect who have done good, they will come to me and will not see death by devouring fire. But the evil creatures, the sinners and the hypocrites will stand in the depths of the darkness that passes not away, and their punishment is the fire, and angels bring forward their sins and prepare for them a place wherein they shall be punished for ever, each according to his offense. The angel of God, Uriel, brings the souls of those sinners who perished in the flood, and of all who dwell in all idols, in every molten image, in every love and in paintings, and of them that dwell on all hills and in stones and by the wayside, whom men call gods: they shall be burned with them in eternal fire. After all of them, with their dwelling places, have been destroyed, they will be punished eternally.

[116–U]   Then will men and women come to the place prepared for them. By their tongues with which they have blasphemed the way of righteousness will they be hung up. There is spread out for them unquenchable fire . . . And behold again another place: this is a great pit filled, in which are those who have denied righteousness; and angels of punishment visit them and here do they kindle upon them the fire of their punishment. And again two women: they are hung up by their neck and by their hair and are cast into the pit. These are they who plaited their hair, not to create beauty, but to turn to fornication, and that they might ensnare the souls of men to destruction. And the men who lay with them in fornication are hung by their thighs in that burning place, and they say to one another, 'We did not know that we would come into everlasting torture.' And the murderers and those who have made common cause with them are cast into the fire, in a place full of venomous beasts, and they are tormented without rest, as they feel their pains, and their worms are as numerous as a dark cloud. And the angel Ezrael will bring forth the souls of them that have been killed and they shall see the torment of those who killed them and shall say to one another, 'Righteousness and justice is the judgment of God. For we have indeed heard, but did not believe that we would come to this place of eternal judgment.'

[117-U]   And near this flame there is a great and very deep pit and into it there flow all kind of things from everywhere: judgment, horrifying things and excretions. And the women are swallowed up by this up to their necks and are punished with great pain. These are they who have procured abortions and have ruined the work of God which he has created. Opposite them is another place where the children sit, but both alive, and they cry to God. And lightnings go forth from those children which pierce the eyes of those who, by fornication, have brought about their desturction. Other men and women stand above them naked. And their children stand opposite to them in a place of delight. And they sigh and cry to God because of their parents, 'These are they who neglected and cursed and transgressed thy commandment. They killed us and cursed the angel who created us and hung us up. And they withheld from us the light which thou hast appointed for all.' And the milk of the mothers flows from their breasts and congeals and smells foul, and from it come forth beasts that devour flesh, which turn and torture them for ever with their husbands, because they forsook the commandment of God and killed their children. And the children shall be given to the angel Temlakos. And those who slew them will be tortured for ever, for God wills it to be so.

[118-U]   Ezrael, the angel of wrath, brings men and women with the half of their bodies burning and casts them into a place of darkness, the hell of men; and a spirit of wrath chastises them with all manner of chastisement, and a worm that never sleeps consumes their entrails. These are the persecutors and betrayers of my righteous ones.

And near to those who live thus were other men and women who chew their tongues, and they are tormented with red hot irons and have their eyes burned. These are the slanderers and those who doubt my righteousness.

Other men and women — whose deeds were done in deception — have their lips cut off and fire enters into their mouths and into their entrails. These are those who slew the martyrs by their lying.

In another place situated near them, on the stone a pillar of fire and the pillar is sharper than swords — men and women who are clad in rags and filthy garments, and they are cast upon it, to suffer the judgment of unceasing torture. These are they which trusted in their riches and despised widows and the woman with orphans . . . in the sight of God.

[119-U]   And into another place near by, saturated with filth, they throw men and women up to their knees. These are they who lent money and took usury. And other men and women thrust themselves down from a high place and return again and run, and demons drive them. These are the worshipers of idols, and they drive them to the end of their wits and they plunge down from there. And this they do continually and are tormented for ever. These are they who have cut their flesh as apostles of a man, and the women who were with them . . . and thus are the men who defiled themselves with one another in the fashion of women. And beside them . . . (an untranslatable word), and beneath them the angel Ezrael prepares a place of much fire, and all the golden and silver idols, all idols, the works of men's hands, and what resembles the images of cats and lions, of reptiles and wild beasts, and the men and women who manufactured the images, shall be in chains of fire; they shall be chastised because of their error before them (the images) and this is their judgment for ever. And near them other men and women who burn in the flame of the judgment, whose torture is for ever. These are they who have forsaken the commandment of God and followed . . . (unknown word) of the devils.

[120-U]   And another very high place . . . (unintelligible words), the men and women who make a false step go rolling down to where the fear is. And again, while the fire that is prepared floweth, they mount up and fall down again and continue their rolling. They shall be punished thus for ever. These are they who have not honored their father and mother, and of their own accord withdrew themselves from them. Therefore shall they be punished eternally. Furthermore the angel Ezrael brings children and maidens to show to them those who are punished. They will be punished with pain, with hanging up and with many wounds which flesh-eating birds inflict. These are they that have confidence in their sins, are not obedient to their parents, and do not follow the instruction of their fathers and do not honor those who are older than they. Beside them, maidens clad in darkness for raiment, and they shall be seriously punished and their flesh will be torn in pieces. These are they who retained not their virginity till they were given in marriage;

they shall be punished with these tortures, while they feel them. And again other men and women who ceaselessly chew their tongues and are tormented with eternal fire. These are the slaves who were not obedient to their masters. This then is their judgment for ever.

[121-U] And near to this torment are blind and dumb men and woman whose raiment is white. They are packed closely together and fall on coals of unquenchable fire. These are they who give alms and say, 'We are righteous before God,' while they yet have not striven for righteousness. The angel of God Ezrael allows them to come forth out of this fire and sets forth a judgment of decision. This then is their judgment. And a stream of fire flows and all those judged are drawn into the midst of the stream. And Uriel sets them down there. And there are wheels of fire, and men and women hung thereon by the power of their whirling. Those in the pit burn. Now these are the sorcerers and sorceresses. These wheels are in all decision by fire without number.

[122-U] The angels will bring my elect and righteous which are perfect in all righteousness, and shall bear them in their hands and clothe them with the garments of eternal life. They shall see their desire in those who hated them, when he punishes them. Torment for every one is for ever according to his deeds. And all those who are in torment will say with one voice, 'Have mercy upon us, for now we know the judgment of God, which he declared to us beforehand, and we did not believe.' And the angel Tatirokos will come and chasten them with even greater torment and will say unto them, 'Now do ye repent when there is no more time for repentance, and nothing of life remains.' And all shall say, 'Righteous is the judgment of God: for we have heard and perceived that his judgment is good, since we are punished according to our deeds.'

[123–U]   Then will I give to my elect and righteous the baptism and the salvation for which they have besought me, in the field Akrōsjā which is called Anēslaslejā. They shall adorn with flowers the portion of the righteous and I will go . . . I will rejoice with them. I will cause the nations to enter into my eternal kingdom and show to them that eternal thing to which I have directed their hope, I and my heavenly Father. I have spoken it to thee, Peter, and make it known to thee. Go forth then and journey to the city in the west in the vineyard which I will tell thee of . . . by the hand of my Son who is without sin, that his work . . . of destruction may be sanctified. But thou art chosen in the hope which I have given to thee.

[124–V]   *When Salome asked, 'How long will death have power?' The Lord answered,* So long as ye women bear children.

[125–V]   *For the Lord himself, on being asked by someone when his kingdom should come, said:* When the two shall be one and that which is without as that which is within, and the male with the female neither male nor female.

[126–X]   In the coming age, *says the Lord,* they will neither marry nor be given in marriage, but will be as the angels in heaven.

Appendices

NOTE ON IDENTIFYING SOURCES

Each of the sayings of Jesus collected in this book is preceded by a number and a letter in brackets. The letters refer to one of the source documents, a total of twenty-four made up of five books of the New Testament, eleven Gnostic Gospels, and eight additional works found in the New Testament Apocrypha. The source of each of Jesus' sayings may therefore be identified by chapter roman numeral, verse number, and source letter — for example, the first saying of Jesus collected in this book ("It is written again, 'You shall not tempt the Lord your God.'") is in chapter I ("Commandments") and identified as [I – A]. Turning to Appendix A: The Gospel of Matthew, one finds under I Commandments, [I – A] 4:7 — meaning The Gospel of Matthew, chapter 4, verse 7. Readers wishing to know the source of the translation of each saying should consult the bibliography and source list at the end of the book.

Appendix A

The Gospel of Matthew

This gospel is traditionally attributed to Matthew, also called Levi, who was a tax collector before becoming a disciple of Jesus. However, it is more probable that many people contributed to the formation of the Gospel. The birth and infancy accounts are peculiar to this gospel and may stem from local oral tradition.

Matthew is based on the Gospel of Mark (the earliest Gospel), which it contains almost in its entirety, and Q (from Quelle, the German word for source), a collection of the sayings of Jesus that scholars believe was used as a source document in the writing of Matthew and Luke. The original text has been estimated to date from as early as 70 C.E. to as late as 95 C.E. It was probably written in Syria, in or around the city of Antioch, since the character of the book seems to reflect the Jewish-Greek background of the church in that city.

References

I – COMMANDMENTS

[1 – A] 4:7	[7 – A] 7:1–2	[13 – A] 18:15–17
[2 – A] 4:10	[8 – A] 7:6	[14 – A] 19:18–21
[3 – A] 4:17	[9 – A] 10:5–7	[15 – A] 22:37–40
[4 – A] 5:33–37	[10 – A] 10:27	[16 – A] 23:8–11
[5 – A] 5:38–45	[11 – A] 11:29–30	[17 – A] 28:19–20
[6 – A] 6:1–4	[12 – A] 16:23–24	

II — PARABLES

[1 – A] 11:16–17	[6 – A] 13:31–32	[11 – A] 13:47–50
[2 – A] 13:3–9	[7 – A] 13:33	[12 – A] 13:52
[3 – A] 13:12	[8 – A] 13:37–43	[13 – A] 15:13–14
[4 – A] 13:19–23	[9 – A] 13:44	[14 – A] 15:17
[5 – A] 13:24–30	[10 – A] 13:45–46	[15 – A] 18:12–14

II – PARABLES (CONTINUED)

[16 – A] 18:23–35	[20 – A] 21:33–41	[24 – A] 24:32–35
[17 – A] 19:23–24	[21 – A] 21:42–44	[25 – A] 25:1–13
[18 – A] 20:1–16	[22 – A] 22:2–10	[26 – A] 25:14–30
[19 – A] 21:28–31	[23 – A] 22:11–14	

III – JESUS SPEAKING ABOUT HIMSELF

[1 – A] 5:17	[6 – A] 13:57	[11 – A] 26:26–28
[2 – A] 8:20	[7 – A] 15:24	[12 – A] 26:61
[3 – A] 9:15	[8 – A] 18:20	[13 – A] 26:64
[4 – A] 12:6	[9 – A] 20:18	[14 – A] 28:18
[5 – A] 12:8	[10 – A] 20:28	

IV – WARNINGS AND ADMONITIONS

[1 – A] 5:19	[13 – A] 12:30	[25 – A] 23:13
[2 – A] 5:21–22	[14 – A] 12:31–33	[26 – A] 23:14
[3 – A] 5:27–28	[15 – A] 12:34–35	[27 – A] 23:15
[4 – A] 6:14–15	[16 – A] 12:43–45	[28 – A] 23:16–17
[5 – A] 6:19–20	[17 – A] 15:11	[29 – A] 23:18–22
[6 – A] 7:13–14	[18 – A] 15:19–20	[30 – A] 23:23–24
[7 – A] 7:21–23	[19 – A] 16:4	[31 – A] 23:25–26
[8 – A] 10:14–15	[20 – A] 16:6	[32 – A] 23:27–28
[9 – A] 10:16–21	[21 – A] 18:7	[33 – A] 23:29–30
[10 – A] 10:29–33	[22 – A] 18:10–11	[34 – A] 26:52
[11 – A] 10:34–39	[23 – A] 19:9	
[12 – A] 11:21–24	[24 – A] 23:12	

V – TEACHINGS AND PROVERBS

[1 – A] 5:3–12	[11 – A] 6:25–26	[21 – A] 9:37–38
[2 – A] 5:14–16	[12 – A] 6:27–30	[22 – A] 10:24–26
[3 – A] 5:18	[13 – A] 6:31–32	[23 – A] 10:40–42
[4 – A] 5:20	[14 – A] 6:33–34	[24 – A] 11:11
[5 – A] 5:23–26	[15 – A] 7:1	[25 – A] 12:48–50
[6 – A] 5:38–41	[16 – A] 7:7–8	[26 – A] 13:15–17
[7 – A] 5:46–48	[17 – A] 7:9–12	[27 – A] 16:2–3
[8 – A] 6:5–6	[18 – A] 7:15–16	[28 – A] 16:24–26
[9 – A] 6:7–8	[19 – A] 8:22	[29 – A] 17:20
[10 – A] 6:22–23	[20 – A] 9:12–13	[30 – A] 18:3–6

V – TEACHINGS AND PROVERBS (CONTINUED)

[31 – A] 18:19   [35 – A] 19:28–30   [39 – A] 22:21
[32 – A] 19:4–6   [36 – A] 20:25–27   [40 – A] 22:31–32
[33 – A] 19:13–14   [37 – A] 21:13   [41 – A] 23:1–4
[34 – A] 19:17   [38 – A] 21:22

VI – HYMNS AND PRAYERS

[1 – A] 6:9–13   [3 – A] 26:39
[2 – A] 11:25–27   [4 – A] 26:42

VIII – DIVERSE DOCTRINE

[1 – A] 4:4   [19 – A] 10:22–23   [37 – A] 17:9–12
[2 – A] 4:19   [20 – A] 11:4–6   [38 – A] 17:17
[3 – A] 5:13   [21 – A] 11:7–10   [39 – A] 17:25–27
[4 – A] 5:29–32   [22 – A] 11:18–19   [40 – A] 18:19–20
[5 – A] 6:16–18   [23 – A] 12:3–5   [41 – A] 19:11–12
[6 – A] 6:24   [24 – A] 12:25–29   [42 – A] 19:26
[7 – A] 7:3–5   [25 – A] 12:36–37   [43 – A] 20:22–23
[8 – A] 7:17–20   [26 – A] 13:13   [44 – A] 21:2–3
[9 – A] 7:24–27   [27 – A] 14:16   [45 – A] 21:13
[10 – A] 8:3–4   [28 – A] 14:27   [46 – A] 21:16
[11 – A] 8:7   [29 – A] 14:31   [47 – A] 21:24–27
[12 – A] 8:10–13   [30 – A] 15:26   [48 – A] 22:41–45
[13 – A] 8:26   [31 – A] 15:28   [49 – A] 26:21
[14 – A] 9:2–6   [32 – A] 15:32   [50 – A] 26:24
[15 – A] 9:16–17   [33 – A] 16:8–11   [51 – A] 26:38
[16 – A] 9:22   [34 – A] 16:13–19   [52 – A] 26:45–46
[17 – A] 9:28–30   [35 – A] 16:27–28   [53 – A] 27:46
[18 – A] 10:8–13   [36 – A] 17:7

IX – APOCALYPTIC AND REVELATION

[1 – A] 17:22–23   [7 – A] 24:12–13   [13 – A] 24:29–30
[2 – A] 24:2   [8 – A] 24:14   [14 – A] 24:31
[3 – A] 24:4–5   [9 – A] 24:15–16   [15 – A] 24:36
[4 – A] 24:6–8   [10 – A] 24:19–22   [16 – A] 24:37–39
[5 – A] 24:9–10   [11 – A] 24:23–24   [17 – A] 24:40–41
[6 – A] 24:11   [12 – A] 24:25–28   [18 – A] 24:42–44

IX − APOCALYPTIC AND REVELATION (CONTINUED)

[19 – A] 24:45–51
[20 – A] 25:31–35
[21 – A] 25:34–40
[22 – A] 25:41–46

Appendix B

The Gospel of Mark

Mark is considered to be the earliest of the four Gospels and was used as a reference by the authors of Matthew and Luke. The Gospel itself is anonymous but tradition states that it was written in Rome by Mark, using the personal recollections of Peter as his guide. It is also the shortest of the New Testament Gospels.

The earliest suggested date for the Gospel is 50 C.E.; 65–67 C.E. is the latest. The latter seems most probable since it was almost certainly written after Peter's death (64–65 C.E.), but in chapter 13, the author seems ignorant of the actual destruction of Jerusalem by Roman armies suppressing the Jewish revolt in 70 C.E. Rome seems the most likely place of origin, since the author uses ten Latin words; and since he explains Jewish traditions and translates Aramaic sayings, it seems obvious he is writing for the Gentiles.

It is generally agreed among scholars that the original work probably ended with chapter 16, verse 8, which portrays the frightened women running from the tomb. The material that follows is thought to have been added by a later scribe or scribes.

References

I – COMMANDMENTS

[18 – B] 6:10–11   [20 – B] 10:19   [22 – B] 12:29–31
[19 – B] 10:14–15   [21 – B] 10:21   [23 – B] 16:15

II – PARABLES

[27 – B] 4:3–9   [30 – B] 4:25   [33 – B] 10:24–25
[28 – B] 4:14–20   [31 – B] 4:26–29   [34 – B] 13:28–31
[29 – B] 4:21–23   [32 – B] 4:30–32

III – JESUS SPEAKING ABOUT HIMSELF

[15 – B] 2:17   [16 – B] 10:45   [17 – B] 13:34

IV – WARNINGS AND ADMONITIONS

[35 – B] 4:24   [38 – B] 7:14–16   [41 – B] 9:42–46
[36 – B] 7:6–8   [39 – B] 8:33   [42 – B] 9:47–50
[37 – B] 7:9–13   [40 – B] 9:38–41   [43 – B] 10:23

V – TEACHINGS AND PROVERBS

[42 – B] 1:17   [48 – B] 9:37   [54 – B] 12:24–25
[43 – B] 2:27–28   [49 – B] 10:26–27   [55 – B] 12:38–40
[44 – B] 7:18–23   [50 – B] 10:29–31   [56 – B] 12:41–44
[45 – B] 8:34–36   [51 – B] 11:22   [57 – B] 16:16–18
[46 – B] 8:38   [52 – B] 11:23
[47 – B] 9:1   [53 – B] 11:24–26

VI – HYMNS AND PRAYERS

[5 – B] 14:36

VII – DIVERSE DOCTRINE

[54 – B] 2:17   [61 – B] 10:5–9   [68 – B] 14:20–21
[55 – B] 4:39   [62 – B] 10:11–12   [69 – B] 14:24–25
[56 – B] 5:36   [63 – B] 10:52   [70 – B] 14:27–28
[57 – B] 8:37   [64 – B] 12:17   [71 – B] 14:38
[58 – B] 9:23   [65 – B] 12:26–27   [72 – B] 14:48–49
[59 – B] 9:31   [66 – B] 13:2   [73 – B] 14:62
[60 – B] 9:35   [67 – B] 14:6–9   [74 – B] 15:34

IX – APOCALYPTIC AND REVELATION

[23 – B] 13:5–6   [27 – B] 13:12–13   [31 – B] 13:21–23
[24 – B] 13:7–8   [28 – B] 13:14–16   [32 – B] 13:24–27
[25 – B] 13:9–10   [29 – B] 13:17–18   [33 – B] 13:32–33
[26 – B] 13:11   [30 – B] 13:19–20   [34 – B] 13:35–37

Appendix C

The Gospel of Luke

The Gospel of Luke is traditionally attributed to Luke, a physician and follower of Paul, although the actual writer or writers remain anonymous. Mostly written in excellent Greek, the document was probably intended for Gentile readers. Luke relied on Mark, Q, a source of his own referred to as L, and the birth and infancy stories. It may be that L and the birth and infancy stories were from oral tradition. Whatever its origin, the writer uses more material from this source than any other, in excess of four hundred verses.

The most likely date for the Gospel is between 70 and 80 C.E. There is a tradition which holds that it was written at Achaia, a Roman province that included northern Greece, but the most probable site is Rome.

The author of Luke also penned the book of Acts, and Luke-Acts combined make up about one-fourth of the New Testament. The rather abrupt ending of Acts in Rome, where Paul awaits his coming trial, also lends credence to the theory that both books were written in that city.

References

I — Commandments

[24 – C] 4:8	[29 – C] 10:3–6	[34 – C] 18:19–20
[25 – C] 6:27–34	[30 – C] 10:28	[35 – C] 21:36
[26 – C] 6:35–38	[31 – C] 12:33–34	[36 – C] 22:25–26
[27 – C] 9:3–5	[32 – C] 14:12–14	
[28 – C] 9:23	[33 – C] 17:3–4	

II — Parables

[35 – C] 5:36–39	[38 – C] 6:43–45	[41 – C] 7:41–43
[36 – C] 6:39–40	[39 – C] 6:46–49	[42 – C] 9:62
[37 – C] 6:41–42	[40 – C] 7:31–32	[43 – C] 10:30–37

II – PARABLES (CONTINUED)

[44 – C] 11:5–8	[51 – C] 14:16–24	[58 – C] 16:1–8
[45 – C] 11:33–36	[52 – C] 14:28–30	[59 – C] 16:13
[46 – C] 12:16–22	[53 – C] 14:31–33	[60 – C] 16:19–31
[47 – C] 12:42–48	[54 – C] 14:34–35	[61 – C] 17:7–10
[48 – C] 13:6–9	[55 – C] 15:4–7	[62 – C] 18:2–8
[49 – C] 13:24–30	[56 – C] 15:8–10	[63 – C] 18:10–14
[50 – C] 14:8–11	[57 – C] 15:11–32	[64 – C] 19:12–27

III – JESUS SPEAKING ABOUT HIMSELF

[18 – C] 4:43	[20 – C] 9:44	[22 – C] 22:27
[19 – C] 9:22	[21 – C] 10:22	

IV – WARNINGS AND ADMONITIONS

[44 – C] 5:31–32	[50 – C] 11:49–51	[56 – C] 12:35–38
[45 – C] 6:24	[51 – C] 11:52	[57 – C] 12:39–40
[46 – C] 6:25	[52 – C] 12:1–3	[58 – C] 12:49
[47 – C] 6:26	[53 – C] 12:4–7	[59 – C] 12:58–59
[48 – C] 11:29–30	[54 – C] 12:8–9	[60 – C] 17:1–2
[49 – C] 11:46	[55 – C] 12:15	

V – TEACHINGS AND PROVERBS

[58 – C] 4:4	[69 – C] 11:11–13	[80 – C] 16:18
[59 – C] 4:12	[70 – C] 11:17	[81 – C] 17:6
[60 – C] 4:18–19	[71 – C] 11:21–22	[82 – C] 17:20–21
[61 – C] 7:24–28	[72 – C] 11:28	[83 – C] 17:24–25
[62 – C] 7:50	[73 – C] 12:14	[84 – C] 18:27
[63 – C] 8:21	[74 – C] 13:33	[85 – C] 19:10
[64 – C] 8:25	[75 – C] 13:34–35	[86 – C] 19:42–44
[65 – C] 10:2	[76 – C] 14:5	[87 – C] 20:34–36
[66 – C] 10:19–20	[77 – C] 16:9–12	[88 – C] 20:37–38
[67 – C] 10:23–24	[78 – C] 16:15	[89 – C] 24:49
[68 – C] 11:9–10	[79 – C] 16:16	

VI – HYMNS AND PRAYERS

[6 – C] 10:21	[7 – C] 11:2–4

VIII – DIVERSE DOCTRINE

[75 – C] 4:24

[76 – C] 6:3–5

[77 – C] 6:20–23

[78 – C] 7:44–48

[79 – C] 9:55–56

[80 – C] 9:60

[81 – C] 11:23–26

[82 – C] 12:10–12

[83 – C] 13:2–3

[84 – C] 14:26–27

[85 – C] 18:16–17

[86 – C] 20:41–44

[87 – C] 21:3–4

[88 – C] 21:33

[89 – C] 22:15–22

[90 – C] 22:36–37

[91 – C] 22:48

[92 – C] 23:34

[93 – C] 23:43

[94 – C] 23:46

[95 – C] 24:25–26

[96 – C] 24:36

[97 – C] 24:38–39

[98 – C] 24:44

[99 – C] 24:46–48

IX – APOCALYPTIC AND REVELATION

[35 – C] 17:20–21

[36 – C] 17:22–23

[37 – C] 17:24–25

[38 – C] 17:26–30

[39 – C] 17:31–32

[40 – C] 17:34–36

[41 – C] 21:6

[42 – C] 21:8–9

[43 – C] 21:10–11

[44 – C] 21:12–15

[45 – C] 21:16–19

[46 – C] 21:20–22

[47 – C] 21:23–24

[48 – C] 21:25–26

[49 – C] 21:27–28

[50 – C] 21:29–31

[51 – C] 21:34–35

Appendix D

The Gospel of John

The Gospel of John was traditionally written by John the son of Zebedee, the disciple whom Jesus loved. The author seems to possess intimate knowledge of Palestine, particully of Jerusalem and the Temple. The work is distinctly Jewish but deliberately lashes out at the Jews, which would seem to indicate it originated after the Christians were expelled from the synagogues, sometime late in the first century.

The Gospel of John contains obvious differences from the synoptic (Greek: *synoptikos*, "having a common view") Gospels (Matthew, Mark, and Luke). Some important events in the synoptic Gospels are not mentioned at all in John, while others happen in different times or places. The differences are probably not intentional but seem to indicate that this Gospel developed independently from the other three.

It is interesting to note that the Jesus of John often seems deliberately vague, conveying more then one meaning at once. To my mind this seems to reflect the Jesus of the Gnostics more than it does the Jesus portrayed in the synoptic Gospels.

References

I – COMMANDMENTS

[37 – D] 6:27	[39 – D] 12:36	[41 – D] 15:12
[38 – D] 7:24	[40 – D] 13:34	[42 – D] 15:17

II – PARABLES

[65 – D] 10:1–5	[67 – D] 10:13–18
[66 – D] 10:7–11	[68 – D] 15:1–6

III – JESUS SPEAKING ABOUT HIMSELF

[23 – D] 2:19

[24 – D] 3:14–15

[25 – D] 3:16–17

[26 – D] 5:19–21

[27 – D] 5:22–23

[28 – D] 5:30–31

[29 – D] 5:39–40

[30 – D] 5:41–43

[31 – D] 6:35

[32 – D] 6:38–39

[33 – D] 6:40

[34 – D] 6:48

[35 – D] 6:51

[36 – D] 7:7–8

[37 – D] 7:16

[38 – D] 7:28–29

[39 – D] 7:33–34

[40 – D] 8:14–16

[41 – D] 8:18

[42 – D] 8:23

[43 – D] 8:26–29

[44 – D] 8:49–51

[45 – D] 8:54–55

[46 – D] 8:58

[47 – D] 9:4–5

[48 – D] 10:25–26

[49 – D] 10:27–29

[50 – D] 10:30

[51 – D] 12:24

[52 – D] 12:26–27

[53 – D] 12:32

[54 – D] 12:44–47

[55 – D] 12:48

[56 – D] 13:13–15

[57 – D] 14:6–7

[58 – D] 14:14–15

[59 – D] 15:13

[60 – D] 16:15–16

[61 – D] 17:11–13

[62 – D] 18:20

IV – WARNINGS AND ADMONITIONS

[6 – D] 12:35

V – TEACHINGS AND PROVERBS

[90 – D] 1:51

[91 – D] 3:3

[92 – D] 3:5–8

[93 – D] 3:11–13

[94 – D] 3:19–21

[95 – D] 4:21

[96 – D] 4:22–24

[97 – D] 4:35–38

[98 – D] 6:32–33

[99 – D] 6:44–46

[100 – D] 6:57–58

[101 – D] 6:62–64

[102 – D] 7:6

[103 – D] 7:18–19

[104 – D] 7:37–38

[105 – D] 8:34–36

[106 – D] 8:38

[107 – D] 8:42–43

[108 – D] 8:44–46

[109 – D] 8:47

[110 – D] 11:9–10

[111 – D] 11:25–26

[112 – D] 12:31

[113 – D] 13:35

[114 – D] 14:1–3

[115 – D] 14:21

[116 – D] 14:23–25

[117 – D] 15:16

[118 – D] 15:18–19

[119 – D] 15:23

[120 – D] 15:26–27

[121 – D] 16:24

[122 – D] 16:32–33

VI – HYMNS AND PRAYERS

[8 – D] 11:41–42

[9 – D] 17:1–26

VIII — DIVERSE DOCTRINE

[100 – D] 4:10

[101 – D] 4:13–14

[102 – D] 4:25–26

[103 – D] 4:48

[104 – D] 5:8

[105 – D] 5:14

[106 – D] 5:24

[107 – D] 5:34–36

[108 – D] 5:44–47

[109 – D] 6:28–29

[110 – D] 6:53–56

[111 – D] 7:21–23

[112 – D] 8:10–11

[113 – D] 8:12

[114 – D] 8:19

[115 – D] 8:21

[116 – D] 8:31–32

[117 – D] 11:40

[118 – D] 12:25

[119 – D] 13:7

[120 – D] 13:10

[121 – D] 13:15–17

[122 – D] 13:18–19

[123 – D] 13:33

[124 – D] 14:9–14

[125 – D] 14:16–20

[126 – D] 14:27–31

[127 – D] 15:7–11

[128 – D] 15:20–22

[129 – D] 15:24–25

[130 – D] 16:23

[131 – D] 18:11

[132 – D] 18:36–37

[133 – D] 19:11

[134 – D] 20:17

[135 – D] 20:21–23

[136 – D] 20:29

[137 – D] 21:18

[138 – D] 21:21–22

IX — APOCALYPTIC AND REVELATION

[52 – D] 16:1–3

[53 – D] 16:7–11

[54 – D] 16:12–14

[55 – D] 16:20–22

Appendix E

The Book of Revelation

Also called the Apocalypse, the Book of Revelation is the only book of a strictly prophetic nature in the New Testament. Although tradition holds that this book was written by the John of the Gospel, most scholars agree that it was probably written by John-Mark, John the Elder, or an as yet unknown John. It seems likely that John was the pastor of the seven churches mentioned, and that he wrote to his brethren to bolster their faith while he was temporarily exiled on the island of Patmos, a Roman penal colony.

The date of origin is the subject of much debate. The earliest suggested date is during the reign of Nero (54–68 C.E.). Although some modern scholars have suggested the reign of Vespasian (69–79 C.E.), another — and some claim better substantiated — view places it during the reign of Domitian (81–96 C.E.).

References

III — JESUS SPEAKING ABOUT HIMSELF

[63 – E] 1:8	[64 – E] 1:17–18	[65 – E] 16:15

IX — APOCALYPTIC AND REVELATION

[56 – E] 2:2–3	[64 – E] 2:18–19	[72 – E] 3:7–8
[57 – E] 2:4–5	[65 – E] 2:20–23	[73 – E] 3:9–10
[58 – E] 2:6–8	[66 – E] 2:24	[74 – E] 3:11
[59 – E] 2:8–9	[67 – E] 2:25–28	[75 – E] 3:12–13
[60 – E] 2:10–11	[68 – E] 3:1	[76 – E] 3:14–16
[61 – E] 2:12–13	[69 – E] 3:2	[77 – E] 3:17–18
[62 – E] 2:14–16	[70 – E] 3:3	[78 – E] 3:19–20
[63 – E] 2:17	[71 – E] 3:4–6	[79 – E] 3:21–22

Appendix F

The Gospel of Thomas

(Gnostic)

A WORD ABOUT THE GNOSTIC TEXTS

The material in appendices F through P has been taken from Gnostic scripture, most of which only came to light in the latter half of this century. The amazing discovery of these texts occurred in 1945 when an Arab peasant decided to dig for fertilizer near a huge boulder, near the town of Nag Hammadi in upper Egypt. During his labor he uncovered a large earthenware jar. Thinking the jar could contain gold, he smashed it only to find a treasure of another sort. The jar contained thirteen ancient papyrus codices. A codex (plural: codices) is an ancient book. Papyrus, parchment, or some other suitable material was stacked and folded down the middle to form the pages, which were sewn onto a leather binding to form a "cover." The cover usually had one or more leather thongs attached in various places that could be wrapped around the codex to keep it closed.

The codices found at Nag Hammadi have come to be known as The Nag Hammadi Library. The fifty-two texts (tractates) contained within are written in Coptic, a common language in Egypt during the early Christian Era, and had been translated from Greek about 1,500 years ago. It is possible that some of these Greek texts were written around the same time as the New Testament Gospels, or even earlier.

Until this discovery in 1945, almost nothing was known of Gnostic beliefs and even less of Gnostic literature. The reasons for this are varied. Then, as now, conflict about specific beliefs and doctrine were common between different Christian sects. For instance, Gnostic thought held that Christ's resurrection was spiritual rather than corporeal, and that the individual must search within to find a sacred path that led to God, a belief not unlike those found in Buddhism. The Gnostics also held that the God of the Jews, and hence the God of other Christian sects, was not the one true God but a deceiver. This violated the bedrock beliefs of the orthodox hierarchy, who insisted that Christ rose "in the flesh" and that the only path to God was through Christ, via the church. Of course, each group felt that they were the "true" followers of Christ and that the others were heretical.

Ultimately, it was the orthodox church as we know it which gained power, and, as so often happens in history, the persecuted became the oppressor. Christian sects not conforming to the orthodox view were condemned and their sacred texts "consigned to the fire." It may have been during one of these purges that a monk or monks (the remains of an ancient monastery are nearby) buried the Nag Hammadi codices rather than see the community's beloved books destroyed.

Before the Nag Hammadi Library was discovered, most knowledge of the Gnostics came from a few scant texts and from the writings of the early church fathers against them. Had it not been for that chance discovery in upper Egypt, most of what we know about the Gnostic movement would be mere conjecture. Instead, the Nag Hammadi texts offer us new insights into early Christianity and a view of Christ from a unique perspective.

THE GOSPEL OF THOMAS

Scholars had long known that a Gospel of Thomas existed during the early Christian era, but the first complete text was only discovered with the Nag Hammadi Library. Although the extant copy is written in Coptic, a common language in Egypt in the early Christian era, the original was undoubtedly written in Greek. Three Greek fragments had been discovered around the turn of the century by

British archeologists in an ancient trash pile at Oxyrhynchus, in upper Egypt. Unfortunately, the scholars sifting through the hundreds of fragments found at Oxyrhynchus had no way to connect them with the Gospel of Thomas, which was thought to be forever lost. It was not until the Nag Hammadi discovery that three of the Oxyrhynchus fragments could be positively identified as coming from the Gospel of Thomas. These fragments contain saying numbers (26–33 and 77:2–3; Prologue and 1–7; and 24 and 36–39) and are identified from the Papyrus Oxyrhynchus as (POxy) 1, 654, and 655, respectively.

The Greek fragments can be dated to about 200 C.E. and the original work may have been written as early as the second half of the first century, around the time the Gospels of the New Testament were being written. There is good evidence to support the earlier date. The Gospel of Thomas has many parallels to the synoptic Gospels and strongly resembles the Q document, which is believed to be a common source of sayings of Jesus used in writing the narrative Gospels of Matthew and Luke. In antiquity, it was common for the students of great philosophers to collect the sayings of their masters in this manner, but this form of collected sayings fell out of favor in Christian circles around 100 C.E., about the same time the narrative Gospels were becoming popular.

In keeping with the Gnostic tradition, the sayings in the Gospel of Thomas were intended to be countercultural. By this I mean they went against the accepted social and political norm of the day. Although the notion of Jesus as countercultural and esoteric may be unfamiliar, it must be remembered that according to the New Testament, the teachings of Jesus were revolutionary in their day, and according to the Gospel of John, even deliberately vague at times.

It can be assumed that the Gospel of Thomas originated in Syria. The Gospel itself states it was written by Didymos Judas Thomas (Didymos and Judas each mean twin; it was believed that Thomas was the twin of Jesus). This form of the name of Thomas was unique to Syria.

The original text was unnumbered. Modern scholars added the numbers for reference.

REFERENCES

I — COMMANDMENTS

[43 – F] #6	[45 – F] #15	[47 – F] #36
[44 – F] #12	[46 – F] #25	[48 – F] #95

II — PARABLES

[69 – F] #8	[76 – F] #45	[83 – F] #76
[70 – F] #9	[77 – F] #47	[84 – F] #96
[71 – F] #20	[78 – F] #57	[85 – F] #97
[72 – F] #21	[79 – F] #63	[86 – F] #98
[73 – F] #33	[80 – F] #64	[87 – F] #103
[74 – F] #35	[81 – F] #65	[88 – F] #107
[75 – F] #40	[82 – F] #75	[89 – F] #109

III — JESUS SPEAKING ABOUT HIMSELF

[66 – F] #10	[72 – F] #31	[78 – F] #77
[67 – F] #13	[73 – F] #38	[79 – F] #82
[68 – F] #16	[74 – F] #43	[80 – F] #86
[69 – F] #17	[75 – F] #52	[81 – F] #90
[70 – F] #28	[76 – F] #62	[82 – F] #104
[71 – F] #30	[77 – F] #71	[83 – F] #108

IV — WARNINGS AND ADMONITIONS

[62 – F] #3	[66 – F] #60	[70 – F] #93
[63 – F] #14	[67 – F] #70	[71 – F] #112
[64 – F] #17	[68 – F] #87	
[65 – F] #27	[69 – F] #89	

V — TEACHINGS AND PROVERBS

[123 – F] #2	[126 – F] #7	[129 – F] #22
[124 – F] #4	[127 – F] #11	[130 – F] #23
[125 – F] #5	[128 – F] #19	[131 – F] #24

V – TEACHINGS AND PROVERBS (CONTINUED)

[132 – F] #26	[147 – F] #55	[162 – F] # 84
[133 – F] #29	[148 – F] #56	[163 – F] #85
[134 – F] #32	[149 – F] #58	[164 – F] #88
[135 – F] #34	[150 – F] #59	[165 – F] #91
[136 – F] #37	[151 – F] #66	[166 – F] #92
[137 – F] #39	[152 – F] #67	[167 – F] #94
[138 – F] #41	[153 – F] #68	[168 – F] #99
[139 – F] #42	[154 – F] #69	[169 – F] #100
[140 – F] #46	[155 – F] #72	[170 – F] #101
[141 – F] #48	[156 – F] #73	[171 – F] #105
[142 – F] #49	[157 – F] #74	[172 – F] #106
[143 – F] #50	[158 – F] #78	[173 – F] #110
[144 – F] #51	[159 – F] #80	[174 – F] #114
[145 – F] #53	[160 – F] #81	
[146 – F] #54	[161 – F] #83	

VIII – DIVERSE DOCTRINE

[139 – F] #1

IX – APOCALYPTIC AND REVELATION

[80 – F] #18	[82 – F] #79	[84 – F] #113
[81 – F] #61	[83 – F] #111	

APPENDIX G

THE APOCRYPHON OF JAMES

Scholars cannot agree on the exact nature of this document. It was originally written in Greek in the late first or early second century, and probably originated in Egypt. Modern scholars gave the document its title, since the original text had none. The document claims to be a secret book (Greek: *apocryphon*) that was revealed to James the Just by Jesus. The work may be based on an early sayings collection.

REFERENCES

I – COMMANDMENTS

[49 – G]7:12–23   [50 – G] 9:19–24   [51 – G] 13:18–26

II – PARABLES

[90 – G] 7:23–26   [92 – G] 12:22–31
[91 – G] 8:11–28   [93 – G] 13:2–8

III – JESUS SPEAKING ABOUT HIMSELF

[84 – G] 12:32–13:1   [85 – G] 14:19–32

IV – WARNINGS AND ADMONITIONS

[72 – G] 3:18–39   [74 – G] 6:2–17   [76 – G] 11:12–12:18
[73 – G] 4:32–5:36   [75 – G] 9:24–10:7   [77 – G] 13:9–18

V – TEACHINGS AND PROVERBS

[175 – G] 2:29–34   [179 – G] 8:29–30   [183 – G] 13:18–26
[176 – G] 3:1–17   [180 – G] 8:33–9:8   [184 – G] 14:5–20
[177 – G] 6:22–31   [181 – G] 10:7–22   [185 – G] 14:38–15:6
[178 – G] 7:18–23   [182 – G] 10:27–11:7

VIII – DIVERSE DOCTRINE

[140 – G] 2:22–27

Appendix H

The Gospel of Philip

The Gospel of Philip is primarily a collection of theological statements concerning Gnostic sacraments. It was probably written in Syria in the late third century and was named for the apostle Philip.

References

IV — WARNINGS AND ADMONITIONS

[78 – H] 57:4–5   [79 – H] 85:30–31

V — TEACHINGS AND PROVERBS

[186 – H] 55:37–56:3   [190 – H] 67:30–35   [194 – H] 77:19
[187 – H] 59:27–28   [191 – H] 68:10–12   [195 – H] 77:26–27
[188 – H] 63:26–31   [192 – H] 72:34–73:1   [196 – H] 78:12
[189 – H] 64:11–13   [193 – H] 74:26–27   [197 – H] 83:13

VII — JESUS LAUGHING

[1 – H] 74:30–35

VIII — DIVERSE DOCTRINE

[141 – H] 58:12–15   [142 – H] 64:2–6

Appendix I

The Book of Thomas the Contender

This work claims to have been written by one calling himself "Mathaias" (possibly meaning Matthew) who overheard the risen Jesus talking with Thomas, whom Jesus calls "brother" and "twin," as they are walking together. It was written in the form of a dialogue, which seems to be a popular style in Gnostic literature. This work was probably written in Syria early in the third century.

References

II – PARABLES

[94 – I] 144:20–37

IV – WARNINGS AND ADMONITIONS

[80 – I] 139:33–140:6	[85 – I] 143:16–17	[90 – I] 144:11–13
[81 – I] 140:9–37	[86 – I] 143:18–19	[91 – I] 144:13–14
[82 – I] 141:3–141:19	[87 – I] 143:19–22	[92 – I] 144:14–20
[83 – I] 142:28–143:9	[88 – I] 143:22–144:2	[93 – I] 144:37–145:1
[84 – I] 143:9–16	[89 – I] 144:9–11	

V – TEACHINGS AND PROVERBS

[198 – I] 138:29–37	[202 – I] 141:26–142:2	[206 – I] 145:6–9
[199 – I] 138:40–139:14	[203 – I] 142:11–19	[207 – I] 145:8–17
[200 – I] 139:22	[204 – I] 145:1–3	
[201 – I] 139:24–32	[205 – I] 145:4–6	

VIII – DIVERSE DOCTRINE

[143 – I] 138:4–21

Appendix J

The Apocalypse of Peter (Gnostic)

This document was written in the third century and purports to be a revelation seen by Peter, as explained by Jesus. The word "apocalypse" is from the Greek word *apokalypsis*, which means a revelation or unveiling. The vision or "revelation" is thought to reveal a secret purpose of God, such as the end of the world and the coming of God's kingdom. The genre is rooted in the prophecy of the Old Testament and was developed between the time of the Old and New Testament. The Book of Revelation in the New Testament is an example of this type of literature.

References

II — PARABLES

[95 – J] 76:5–18

IV — WARNINGS AND ADMONITIONS

[94 – J] 81:29–82:3

V — TEACHINGS AND PROVERBS

[208 – J] 70:21–72:5	[211 – J] 76:19–77:22	[214 – J] 83:16–84:12
[209 – J] 72:10	[212 – J] 79:23–32	
[210 – J] 75:8–76:4	[213 – J] 80:9–24	

VII — JESUS LAUGHING

[7 – J] 81:16–19	[8 – J] 82:4–5	[9 – J] 82:27–83:3

VIII — DIVERSE DOCTRINE

[144 – J] 71:6–72:3	[145 – J] 72:10–73:11	[146 – J] 78:32–79:22

IX — APOCALYPTIC AND REVELATION

[85 – J] 73:23–75:8   [87 – J] 78:32–79:22

[86 – J] 77:23–78:32   [88 – J] 80:24–81:3

Appendix K

The Gospel of Mary

The original text may have been written in Syria or Egypt in the late first or early second century. The most complete text, the Coptic, has been dated to the early fifth century, and there are two Greek fragments that have been dated to the third century. The Coptic text found at Nag Hammadi is missing pages (possibly as many as ten), which may comprise as much as half of the entire work.

Since Mary takes a role of authority in this work, it may reflect the willingness of some early Christians to see women in leadership roles.

References

IV — WARNINGS AND ADMONITIONS
[95 – K] 8:13–9:5

V — TEACHINGS AND PROVERBS
[215 – K] 7:3–10   [216 – K] 7:14–21   [217 – K] 10:15–16

Appendix L

The Exegesis on the Soul

Although we know only the Coptic version, the original was probably written in Greek sometime in the early second century. The text gives an account of the tribulations of a mythical soul, and uses religious allusions and quotes from Greek mythology to illustrate and support the narrative.

References

V – teachings and proverbs

[218 – L] 134:36–135:5   [219 – L] 135:17–19   [220 – L] 135:19–21

Appendix M

The Dialogue of the Savior

The dating of this fragmentary tractate is a matter of debate, but some of the dialogue seems to be based on a collection of sayings that resemble Q. As in the Gospel of Mary, Mary Magdalene is praised and chosen to receive special teaching with two other disciples.

References

IV – WARNINGS AND ADMONITIONS
[96 – M] 142:12–16

V – TEACHINGS AND PROVERBS

[221 – M] 120:1–8   [224 – M] 140:12–15   [227 – M] 142:7
[222 – M] 126:8–11   [225 – M] 141:9–13   [228 – M] 144:16–17
[223 – M] 126:14–17   [226 – M] 141:15–20

VI – HYMNS AND PRAYERS
[10 – M] 121:5–122:1

Appendix N

The Sophia of Jesus Christ

The Sophia of Jesus Christ is a Christianized version of an older, non-Christian work known as "Eugnostos the Blessed." The tractate blends several different theologies in the Gnostic tradition. The original work was probably written in Greek and originated sometime in the first two centuries.

References

III — Jesus Speaking about Himself

[86 – N] 94:5–14   [88 – N] 121:14–III 117:9
[87 – N] 107:12–108:5   [89 – N] 118:16–119:9

IV — Warnings and Admonitions

[97 – N] 98:1–10

V — Teachings and Proverbs

[229 – N] 91:22–23   [236 – N] 102:21–103:22   [242 – N] B.G. 107:17–
[230 – N] 92:7–93:5   [237 – N] 104:6–105:2   112:20
[231 – N] 95:22–96:14   [238 – N] 105:9–106:10   [243 – N] 114:13–
[232 – N] 97:19–24   [239 – N] 106:15–107:12   B.G. 121:14
[233 – N] 98:12–23   [240 – N] 108:5–16   [244 – N] 117:9–118:2
[234 – N] 98:23–99:14   [241 – N] 108:19–   [245 – N] 118:3–118:16
[235 – N] 100:19–102:20   B.G. 107:14

VII — Jesus Laughing

[10 – N] 91:25–92:2

VIII — Diverse Doctrine

[147 – N] B.G. 84:13–95:19   [148 – N] 96:19–97:18   [149 – N] 98:14–23

Appendix O

The Second Treatise of the Great Seth

The Second Treatise of the Great Seth is a Gnostic Christian work in the form of a dialogue allegedly spoken by Jesus Christ. It presents the Gnostic belief that the God of the Old Testament and his prophets are laughingstocks because he is a counterfeit and ignorant being, far below "the Father of Truth," who is the true God. The treatise describes the descent of Jesus from this true heaven, through the lower regions of the heavens, down to Earth and back again. Like most Gnostic texts, it teaches that salvation is to be gained through knowledge.

Regardless of the title, the name "Seth" does not appear in the dialogue at all. However, it is possible that "Seth" is meant to be identified with Jesus.

References

III — JESUS SPEAKING ABOUT HIMSELF

[90 – O] 49–50:1
[91 – O] 51:21–52:10
[92 – O] 54:14–56:20
[93 – O] 56:21–57:20
[94 – O] 65:19–33
[95 – O] 67:19–68:28

IV — WARNINGS AND ADMONITIONS

[98 – O] 59:19–60:13
[99 – O] 65:2–19

V — TEACHINGS AND PROVERBS

[246 – O] 61:16–62:26

VII — JESUS LAUGHING

[2 – O] 53:32–34
[3 – O] 56:19–20

VIII – DIVERSE DOCTRINE

Appendix P

The Apocryphon of John

The Apocryphon of John is a Gnostic work dating from around 185 C.E. in its earliest form. The book was still in use in Mesopotamia as late as the eighth century C.E. Only three quotes from the Apocryphon of John are used in this work. All three can be found in chapter 7, "Jesus Laughing."

References

VII — JESUS LAUGHING

[4 – P] 13:19–24   [5 – P] 22:12–16   [6 – P] 26:25–29

APPENDIX Q

EPISTULA APOSTOLORUM

Appendices Q through X represent apocryphal works. Although some of the works express Gnostic tendencies, most of these texts were popular within the early church. Unlike the true Gnostic works, these writings were generally not considered heretical by the early orthodox church and were considered beneficial for secular reading.

The existence of this work was unknown until 1895, when fifteen leaves of the text, in Coptic, were discovered in Cairo, Egypt. The entire text was later found in an Ethiopic translation and was first published in 1919. Written in the first half of the second century, it seems to be written from an orthodox point of view but is heavily influenced by Gnostic thought. It is probably this borrowing of Gnostic ideas that caused the work to be dropped from orthodox Christianity.

REFERENCES

I — COMMANDMENTS

[52 – Q] 15:4–6	[55 – Q] 30:3–6	[58 – Q] 46
[53 – Q] 18:2–19:4	[56 – Q] 30:7	[59 – Q] 51:6
[54 – Q] 19:4–7	[57 – Q] 41:1	

II — PARABLES;

[96 – Q] 32:14–15	[97 – Q] From 42–43	[98 – Q] From 43:44

III — JESUS SPEAKING ABOUT HIMSELF

[96 – Q] From 10	[100 – Q] 16	[104 – Q] From 21
[97 – Q] From 11	[101 – Q] From 17	[105 – Q] From 21
[98 – Q] 13	[102 – Q] From 19	
[99 – Q] From 14	[103 – Q] From 19	

IV – WARNINGS AND ADMONITIONS

[100 – Q] From 24   [102 – Q] From 29   [104 – Q] 47
[101 – Q] 27   [103 – Q] From 39   [105 – Q] From 50

V – TEACHINGS AND PROVERBS

[247 – Q] 15   [254 – Q] From 29   [261 – Q] From 39–40
[248 – Q] From 19:7   [255 – Q] From 30   [262 – Q] From 41
[249 – Q] From 21   [256 – Q] From 32   [263 – Q] From 42
[250 – Q] From 24   [257 – Q] From 36   [264 – Q] 48–49
[251 – Q] From 25   [258 – Q] From 36   [265 – Q] From 50
[252 – Q] From 28   [259 – Q] 38
[253 – Q] From 28   [260 – Q] From 39

IX – APOCALYPTIC AND REVELATION

[89 – Q] 17:1   [94 – Q] 29:9   [99 – Q] From 36
[90 – Q] From 19   [95 – Q] 31   [100 – Q] From 37
[91 – Q] From 19   [96 – Q] 33   [101 – Q] From 39
[92 – Q] 25–26   [97 – Q] From 34   [102 – Q] From 50
[93 – Q] 29:2   [98 – Q] 35

Appendix R

The Acts of John

The original text was probably written in Asia Minor sometime in the second or third century C.E.; the traditional writer is one Leucius Charinus. The text was known to the church fathers and has come to us in several languages. Its survival is surprising since the Nicene Council of 787 C.E. decreed that it was one of the books that deserved to be "consigned to the fire," and forbade copying or owning the work. Although extant in several fragmented translations, it has been estimated that as much as half the work may still be lost.

This work has also been heavily influenced by Gnostic thought, which led to its renunciation by the orthodox church.

References

III — Jesus Speaking About Himself

[106 – R] 101

V — Teachings and Proverbs

[266 – R] From 92	[268 – R] From 98	[270 – R] 100
[267 – R] From 97	[269 – R] From 99	[271 – R] From 101

VI — Hymns and Prayers

[11 – R] 94–96

Appendix S

The Gospel of Bartholomew

This work is preserved in Greek, Latin, Slavonic, and Coptic fragments. This narrative comes from the third century C.E. and, like much of the literature from that time, has been influenced by Gnostic tradition and has many parallels to the Gnostic gospels.

References

III — JESUS SPEAKING ABOUT HIMSELF

[107 – S] 1:1–2   [108 – S] IV 65

IV — WARNINGS AND ADMONITIONS

[106 – S] 1–2

V — TEACHINGS AND PROVERBS

[272 – S] I 1:5   [275 – S] From II 7   [278 – S] III 21
[273 – S] I 1:26–27   [276 – S] III 3   [279 – S] III 66–68
[274 – S] I 1:28–34   [277 – S] III 18–19

VI — HYMNS AND PRAYERS

[12 – S] IV 70

Appendix T

The Apocalypse of Thomas

Written in the fifth century C.E. or before, the Apocalypse of Thomas is related to, and dependent on, the Johannine Book of Revelation in the New Testament. Here, as in Revelation, the number seven plays a prominent role as the work shows the last seven days leading to the end of the world. Two versions have survived to the present; both texts exhibit a blend of Orthodox and Gnostic beliefs.

Numbers [103 – T] to [110 – T], listed in Chapter IX "Apocalyptic and Revelation," represent the work, which is unnumbered, in its entirety.

IX — APOCALYPTIC AND REVELATION

[103 – T]   [106 – T]   [109 – T]
[104 – T]   [107 – T]   [110 – T]
[105 – T]   [108 – T]

Appendix U

The Apocalypse of Peter (Ethiopic)

The Apocalypse of Peter is a sadistic drama showing not the salvation that can be found through Christ, but the punishment of those who are not saved.

The work has been known since 1887, when a Greek fragment was uncovered in Egypt in the grave of a Christian monk; an Ethiopic version was discovered in 1910. It can be dated from at least the first half of the second century c.e. and seems to have been popular among early Christians. Egypt has been suggested as the place of origin.

This work should not be confused with the Gnostic text, discovered in 1945 in Nag Hammadi, that bears the same title.

References

I – COMMANDMENTS
[60 – U] 14

II – PARABLES
[99 – U] 2   [100 – U] 4

IV – WARNINGS AND ADMONITIONS
[107 – U] From 1   [108 – U] From 3   [109 – U] From 16

V – TEACHINGS AND PROVERBS
[280 – U] From 16

VIII – DIVERSE DOCTRINE
[160 – U] From 15

IX – APOCALYPTIC AND REVELATION

[111 – U] 1:3–12

[112 – U] From 2

[113 – U] From 4

[114 – U] 5

[115 – U] 6

[116 – U] 7

[117 – U] 8

[118 – U] 9

[119 – U] 10

[120 – U] 11

[121 – U] 12

[122 – U] 13

[123 – U] From 14

APPENDIX V

CLEMENT OF ALEXANDRIA [145–220 C.E.?)

Possibly the most original thinker in the Ante–Nicene church was Clement of Alexandria. Almost nothing is known of his life, except that he may have been Greek and probably came from Athens. Regarded as a Christian Platonist, he was the first Christian writer to assert the doctrine of free will.

The four references from Clement of Alexandria in this book all come from his work the "Stromateis."

PSEUDO–CLEMENT

The so-called "Second Epistle of Clement" has no heading and for centuries was erroneously attributed to Clement of Rome (an earlier authority, unrelated to Clement of Alexandria). Although the exact date of the work is not known, it certainly belongs to an early period of the church, a probable date being between 100 and 140 C.E.

REFERENCES

I – COMMANDMENTS
[61 – V] From Stromateis III

III – JESUS SPEAKING ABOUT HIMSELF
[109 – V] From Stromateis III

IV – WARNINGS AND ADMONITIONS
[110 – V]2nd Clem. 4, 5
[111 – V] 2nd Clem. 8, 5

V — TEACHINGS AND PROVERBS

[281 – V] From Stromateis III
[282 – V] 2nd Clem. 5, 2–4
[283 – V] 2nd Clem. 9, 11

IX — APOCALYPTIC AND REVELATION

[124 – V] From Stromateis III
[125 – V] 2nd Clem. 12,1–2

Appendix W

The Kerygmata Petrou

There are only three references from the Kerygmata Petrou in this work, and all three are in "Teachings and Proverbs." The Kerygmata Petrou is in a very fragmented form. The original order of the fragments is a matter of conjecture. The work may be related to Luke-Acts of the New Testament. Clement of Alexandria knew of the work and quoted from it, believing it to be composed by the Apostle Peter. Dates for its origin range between 80 and 140 C.E.

References

V – Teachings and Proverbs

[284 – W] From 5, H III 50
[285 – W] From 5, H III 50
[286 – W] From 5, H III 50

Appendix X

Epistle of Titus, the Disciple of Paul on the State of Chastity

This text was discovered in 1896 in a Latin manuscript dating from the eighth century, and may originate as late as the fifth century. It contains references to many apocryphal writings as well as passages from the scriptures. A life of chastity and asceticism is stressed. Its origin and its author are both unknown.

The nine references in this work are contained in the three sections listed below. There are no chapter and verse references in this text.

References

IV — WARNINGS AND ADMONITIONS

[112 – X]   [113 – X]

V — TEACHINGS AND PROVERBS

[287 – X]   [289 – X]   [291 – X]
[288 – X]   [290 – X]   [292 – X]

IX — APOCALYPTIC AND REVELATION

[126 – X]

Afterword

Jesus Laughing

Since the references from chapter 7, "Jesus Laughing," are not listed in one appendix but come from various appendices throughout the book, I have listed them below in order of appearance in this work for the sake of convenience. Since this list does not follow the standard reference style I have used throughout the rest of this work, I have given the title of the tractate as well as its numerical reference.

[1–H]   From The Gospel of Philip. 74:29, 34
[2–J]   From The Apocalypse of Peter (Gnostic) 81:16, 19
[3–J]   From The Apocalypse of Peter (Gnostic) 82:4, 5
[4–J]   From The Apocalypse of Peter (Gnostic) 82:27–83:3
[5–N]   From The Sophia of Jesus Christ. 91:25–92:2
[6–O]   From The Second Treatise of the Great Seth. 53:32, 34
[7–O]   From The Second Treatise of the Great Seth. 56:19, 20
[8–P]   From The Apocryphon of John. 13:19, 24
[9–P]   From The Apocryphon of John. 22:12, 16
[10–P] From The Apocryphon of John. 26:25, 29

Glossary

Aeons	One of the ruling beings in the Gnostic Pleroma or one of the powers created by Yaldabaoth.
Apocryphon	A secret book. Presumably containing teachings and revelations not generally known.
Archons	Also called "rulers" and "authorities." They are seen as the spirit rulers of the Earth and planets. The Hebrew God is sometimes called "The First Archon." The archons (including the Hebrew God) were considered evil by the Gnostics.
Barbelo	Sometimes associated with Sophia and sometimes as one of the powers in the threefold nature of God.
Boundless One	The true all-powerful God.
Charis	Spirit.
Cosmocrator	The Gnostic false god of this world. *See* Demiurge.
Demiurge	The God of the Hebrews and of creation in Gnostic belief. He was considered evil by the Gnostics since he claimed to be the only God, but was actually under the authority of the Highest God.
Ennoia	Thought.
First Existing One	A name given by the Gnostics to the true God.
Gnosis	Knowledge.
Hebdomad	The seventh.
Judas Thomas	Sometimes just Thomas. Believed by the Gnostics to be the twin brother of Jesus.
Logos	Word.

Monad	The Father of everything.
Nous	The mind or first emanation from God.
Ogdoad	Eight. Beyond the Hebdomad. The first eight Aeons of the Pleroma.
Parousia	Arrival or coming. Used in Christianity to denote the second coming of Christ.
Pistis	Faith. Usually associated with Sophia.
Pleroma	The highest Aeons that make up the attributes of the true God. The heavens or the beings who exist there.
Seth	The third son of Adam and Eve.
Sophia	Wisdom. One of the Pleroma that emanated from the True God. In Gnostic tradition she brings forth the Demiurge.
Tractate	A single text contained with other works in a codex or book. A tractate is a complete work in itself.
Yaldabaoth	Also written Ialdabaoth — one of the Gnostic names for the ignorant and false God. *See* Demiurge.

Suggested Reading

The OTHER Bible
Edited by Willis Barnstone
Copyright 1984. HarperCollins Publishers.

The Historical Jesus: The Life of a Mediterranean Jewish Peasant
By John Dominic Crossan
Copyright 1991. HarperCollins Publishers, Harper San Francisco.

The Laughing Savior
By John Dart
Copyright 1976. Harper & Row Publishers.

Jesus: An Historian's Review of the Gospels
By Michael Grant
Copyright 1977. Michael Grant Publications Ltd.

The Complete Gospels
Edited by Robert J. Miller
Copyright 1992, 1994. HarperCollins Publishers.

The Gnostic Gospels
By Elaine Pagels
Copyright 1979. Random House.

Jesus the Magician
By Morton Smith
Copyright 1978. Harper & Row Publishers, Inc.

A History of the Early Church to A.D. 500
by J. W. C. Wand
Copyright 1937. Reprinted 1977, 1979. Methuen & Co.

Bibliography and Sources

New Testament Apocrypha Volume I and II (NTA). By Edgar Hennecke. Edited by Wilhelm Scheemelcher. English translation (from German) by R. McL. Wilson. Copyright 1959, J. C. B . Mohr (Paul Siebeck), Tübingen. English translation: vol. I, copyright 1963; vol. II, copyright 1965 by Lutterworth Press. Published by Westminster Press, Philadelphia, Pennsylvania. Originally published in 1959 as *Neutestamentliche Apokryphen* by J. C. B. Mohr, Tübingen, Germany.

Epistula Apostolorum (NTA) vol. I, pp. 189-227. Translated by H. Duensing.

The Acts of John (NTA) vol. II, pp. 215-258 and sections from The Hymn of Jesus (HOJ) (see below).

The Gospel of Bartholomew (NTA) vol. I, pp. 484-503. Translated by F. Scheidweiler.

Apocalypse of Thomas (NTA) vol. II, pp. 799-803. Translated by A. de Santos Otero.

Apocalypse of Peter (Ethiopic) (NTA) vol. II, pp. 668-683. Translated by H. Duensing.

Fragments of Clement of Alexandria and 2nd Clement (NTA) vol. I, pp. 166-178.

The Kerygmata Petrou (NTA) vol. II, pp. 102-127. Translated by W. Schneemelcher.

Epistle of Titus, the Disciple of Paul (NTA) vol. II, pp. 145-166. Translated by A. de Santos Otero.

The Nag Hammadi Library in English (NHL). Translated by: Members of the Coptic Gnostic Library Project of the Institute of Antiquity and Christianity. James M. Robinson, Director. Copyright 1977 by E. J. Brill, Leiden, The Netherlands. Harper and Row, Publishers, Inc., 10 East 53rd St., New York, NY.

The Gospel of Thomas (NHL), pp. 118-130. Translated by Thomas O. Lambdin. The numeration of 114 sayings is not in the original manuscript but is followed by most scholars today.

Apocalypse of Peter (Gnostic) (NHL) pp. 340-345. Translated by Roger A. Bullard.

The Gospel of Mary (NHL) pp. 471-474. Translated by George W. MacRae and R. McL. Wilson.

The Exegesis of the Soul (NHL) pp. 180-187. Translated by William C. Robinson, Jr.

The Dialogue of the Savior (NHL) pp. 230-238. Translated by Harold W. Attridge.

The Sophia of Jesus Christ (NHL) pp. 207-228, translated by Douglas M. Parrott.

The Apocryphon of James (NHL) pp. 29-36. Translated by Francis E. Williams.

The Gospel of Philip (NHL) pp. 131–151. Translated by Wesley W. Isenberg.

The Book of Thomas the Contender (NHL) pp. 188-194. Translated by John D. Turner.

The Second Treatise of the Great Seth (NHL) pp. 330-338. Translated by Roger A. Bullard.

The Apocryphon of John (NHL) pp. 98-116. Translated by Frederik Wisse.

The Hymn of Jesus (HOJ). Translated by G. R. S. Mead. First printing 1907, second impression 1963. Published by John M. Watkins, 21 Cecil Court, Charing Cross Road, Clackmannashire, Great Britain. *Note:* Pages 21–25 contained within "Hymns and Prayers."

BIBLES

King James Version

Copyright 1984, 1977, Thomas Nelson Publishers

All verses in this work from Revelation; six verses from Matthew.

The New King James Version

Copyright 1982, Thomas Nelson Publishers

All verses in this work from the Gospels of Matthew (excluding six
verses) and Luke.

The New Oxford Annotated Bible

Revised Standard Version

Copyright 1971, Oxford University Press.

All verses in this work from the Gospels of Mark and John.